The Letter to the Hebrews contains the most important explanation of the sacrificial death of Christ in the New Testament. In this book, which is intended for both students and general readers, Barnabas Lindars explains the circumstances in which Hebrews was written, and expounds the writer's argument at length. At each stage of the survey, the writer's ideas are related to the main topics of New Testament theology. Special attention is paid to the rhetorical style of Hebrews, which marks it out as having been written in response to an urgent practical situation. The concluding chapters show the place of Hebrews in the context of the development of early Christianity, and indicate the lasting value of Hebrews for theology today.

NEW TESTAMENT THEOLOGY

General Editor: Professor J. D. G. Dunn,
Department of Theology, University of Durham

The theology of the Letter to the Hebrews

This series provides a programmatic survey of the individual writings of the New Testament. It aims to remedy the deficiency of available published material, which has tended to concentrate on historical, textual, grammatical, and literary issues at the expense of the theology, or to lose distinctive emphases of individual writings in systematised studies of 'The Theology of Paul' and the like. New Testament specialists here write at greater length than is usually possible in the introductions to commentaries or as part of other New Testament theologies, and explore the theological themes and issues of their chosen books without being tied to a commentary format, or to a thematic structure drawn from elsewhere. When complete, the series will cover all the New Testament writings, and will thus provide an attractive, and timely, range of texts around which courses can be developed.

THE THEOLOGY OF THE
LETTER TO THE HEBREWS

BARNABAS LINDARS, SSF

*Emeritus Professor of Biblical Criticism
and Exegesis,
University of Manchester*

CAMBRIDGE
UNIVERSITY PRESS

CAMBRIDGE UNIVERSITY PRESS
Cambridge, New York, Melbourne, Madrid, Cape Town, Singapore, São Paulo

Cambridge University Press
The Edinburgh Building, Cambridge CB2 2RU, UK

Published in the United States of America by Cambridge University Press, New York

www.cambridge.org
Information on this title: www.cambridge.org/9780521354875

© Cambridge University Press 1991

First published 1991
Reprinted 1994, 1995, 1997, 1999, 2001, 2003

A catalogue record for this publication is available from the British Library

Library of Congress Cataloguing in Publication data
Lindars, Barnabas
The theology of the Letter to the Hebrews / Barnabas Lindars.
p.   cm. – (New Testament theology)
Includes bibliographical references and indexes.
ISBN 0 521 35487 0. – ISBN 0 521 35748 9 (pbk.)
1. Bible. N. T. Hebrews – Theology.
2. Bible. N. T. Hebrews – Critiscism, interpretation, etc.
I. Title.   II. Series.
BS2775.5.L55   1991
227′.8706 – dc20   90–43044   CIP

ISBN-13 978-0-521-35487-5 hardback
ISBN-10 0-521-35487-0 hardback

ISBN-13 978-0-521-35748-7 paperback
ISBN-10 0-521-35748-9 paperback

Transferred to digital printing 2006

Contents

CONTENTS

Editor's preface

Although the New Testament is usually taught within Departments or Schools or Faculties of Theology/Divinity/Religion, theological study of the individual New Testament writings is often minimal or at best patchy. The reasons for this are not hard to discern.

For one thing, the traditional style of studying a New Testament document is by means of straight exegesis, often verse by verse. Theological concerns jostle with interesting historical, textual, grammatical and literary issues, often at the cost of the theological. Such exegesis is usually very time-consuming, so that only one or two key writings can be treated in any depth within a crowded three-year syllabus.

For another, there is a marked lack of suitable textbooks round which courses could be developed. Commentaries are likely to lose theological comment within a mass of other detail in the same way as exegetical lectures. The section on the theology of a document in the Introduction to a commentary is often very brief and may do little more than pick out elements within the writing under a sequence of headings drawn from systematic theology. Excursuses usually deal with only one or two selected topics. Likewise larger works on New Testament Theology usually treat Paul's letters as a whole and, having devoted the great bulk of their space to Jesus, Paul and John, can spare only a few pages for others.

In consequence, there is little incentive on the part of teacher or student to engage with a particular New Testament document, and students have to be content with a general overview, at best complemented by in-depth study of (parts of) two or three New Testament writings. A serious corollary to this is the degree to which students are thereby incapacitated in the task of integrating their New Testament study with the rest of their Theology or Religion courses, since often they are capable only of drawing on the general overview or on a sequence of particular verses treated atomistically. The growing importance of a literary-critical approach to individual documents simply highlights the present deficiencies even more. Having been given little experience in handling individual New Testament writings as such at a theological level, most students are very ill prepared to develop a properly integrated literary and theological response to particular texts. Ordinands too need more help than they currently receive from textbooks, so that their preaching from particular passages may be better informed theologically.

There is need therefore for a series to bridge the gap between too brief introduction and too full a commentary where theological discussion is lost among too many other concerns. It is our aim to provide such a series. That is, a series where New Testament specialists are able to write at greater length on the theology of individual writings than is usually possible in the introductions to commentaries or as part of New Testament Theologies, and to explore the theological themes and issues of these writings without being tied to a commentary format or to a thematic structure provided from elsewhere. The volumes seek both to describe each document's theology, and to engage theologically with it, noting also its canonical context and any specific influence it may have had on the history of Christian faith and life. They are directed at those who already have one or two years of full-time New Testament and theological study behind them.

James D. G. Dunn
University of Durham

Preface

The Letter to the Hebrews is so obviously full of theology that the main problem is not how to dig it out, but how to present it in an assimilable form. In preparing this book I considered the possibility of a systematic treatment, dealing with all the standard topics of theology in a logical order. I decided against this on the grounds that the theology of Hebrews is related to a sustained argument, which runs through the letter from start to finish. This argument is not a theological treatise, but an urgent address to the original readers, who are on the brink of taking action which their leaders regard as nothing short of apostasy. The author uses his considerable rhetorical skill as a writer to persuade them to change their minds. Consequently his theology is liable to be misrepresented if it is detached from the context in which it is used. I have therefore adhered closely to the order of the text, except that Hebrews 13, which provides the clues for understanding the situation of the readers, is dealt with at the beginning.

This explains why the subjects are taken in a seemingly illogical order, why some subjects receive what may be regarded as disproportionate attention, and some subjects little or no attention at all. Thus there is no section on the doctrine of God in Hebrews. This is because Hebrews takes for granted the monotheistic idea of God common to Judaism and earliest Christianity. Special features of his doctrine of God are covered by what is said in the sections on christology and the Holy Spirit. Those who wish to follow up particular aspects of the theology of Hebrews should consult the index of subjects.

It will already be apparent that the designation 'Hebrews' is

used in more than one way in this book. Very often it means the
letter itself, and so is referred to by the pronoun 'it'. But it is
also used to denote the author, because the true name of the
author is unknown. In this case the pronoun is 'he'. The
masculine pronoun is used for convenience, and does not
preclude the possibility that the letter was written by a woman.
This allows for a little ambiguity, for example the theology of
Hebrews means both the theology of the author and the
theology which is contained in the letter. Of course there is no
real difference between them. In addition 'the Hebrews
church' and 'the Hebrews community' mean the people to
whom the letter is addressed regardless of any theory of their
identity. In all three usages 'Hebrews' always has the plural
form, though it is treated as singular. In other words it is just a
name for the author, the letter and the receiving community.
The use of it in these ways does not imply any particular theory
about why or how 'To the Hebrews' became attached to the
letter as its heading in the manuscripts.

It has been a pleasure to write this book, because Hebrews is
so interesting and inspiring. Approaching it with an eye to the
rhetorical effects helped to bring out the author's personality
and to reveal a far more attractive personality than one may
expect at first glance. Hebrews is rather like the prophet
Ezekiel. He appears strange and impersonal and distant at
first, but closer acquaintance shows him to be a deeply caring
person with a strong pastoral sense. In fact Hebrews' concept
of the pastoral character of priesthood is one of the points of
lasting value in this very distinctive New Testament writing.

This book began as a series of lectures to a small but
enthusiastic class of Extra-Mural Studies in Manchester, and I
am grateful to the students for the encouragement of their
response.

Abbreviations

AV	Authorised Version
B	Codex Vaticanus (fourth century)
BAG	W. Bauer, W. F. Arndt, and F. W. Gingrich, *A Greek–English Lexicon of the New Testament* (Cambridge, 1952)
Barn.	*Epistle of Barnabas*
CD	The Damascus Document from the Cairo Genizah
1 *Clem.*	The genuine *Epistle of Clement* of Rome
Clement, *Strom.*	The *Stromateis* (miscellanies) of Clement of Alexandria
D	Codex Bezae (fifth century). D^* = first hand of D
d	Latin side of Codex Bezae (Old Latin text)
Epiphanius, *Pan.*	Epiphanius, *Against all the Heresies*
Euseb., *H.E.*	Eusebius, *Ecclesiastical History*
JBL	*Journal of Biblical Literature*
Josephus, *Ant.*	Josephus, *Antiquities of the Jews*
War.	*Jewish War*
JTS	*Journal of Theological Studies* (new series)
Jub.	*Book of Jubilees*
Justin, I *Ap.*	Justin Martyr, *First Apology*
LXX	The Septuagint (Greek) version of the OT
MM	J. H. Moulton and G. Milligan, *The Vocabulary of the Greek Testament* (London, 1914–29)

MS(S)	Manuscript(s)
NEB	New English Bible
NovT	*Novum Testamentum*
NRT	*Nouvelle Revue Théologique*
NT	New Testament
NTS	*New Testament Studies*
OT	Old Testament
P	ninth-century Greek MS
P⁴⁶	Papyrus Chester Beatty II (about AD 200), the oldest MS containing Hebrews
Philo, *de Ebr.*	Philo Judaeus, *On the Drunkenness of Noah*
Leg. All.	*Allegory of the Laws*
de Migr. Abr.	*On the Migration of Abraham*
Quaest. in Gen.	*Questions on Genesis*
1Q, 4Q, 5Q, 11Q	Document from Qumran Cave 1, Cave 4, etc., followed by name or number of the document
1QS	The Manual of Discipline from Cave 1
1QSᵃ	The Messianic Rule appended to 1QS
4QpIsaᵈ	Fourth fragment of commentary on Isaiah from Cave 4
RB	*Revue Biblique*
RSV	Revised Standard Version
RSVm	Revised Standard Version margin
RQ	*Revue de Qumran*
RV	Revised Version
s.v.	sub voce
sy⁽ᵖ⁾·ʰ	Syriac version. (p) = the reading in question is partly supported by the Syriac Peshitta. h = Harkleian Syriac
TDNT	*Theological Dictionary of the New Testament*, ed. G. Kittel and G. Friedrich, trans. G. W. Bromiley (9 vols., Grand Rapids, 1964–74).
UBS	United Bible Societies' text of the Greek NT
1739	tenth-century Greek MS

CHAPTER I

The historical setting of Hebrews

INTRODUCTION

The author of Hebrews ranks with Paul and the Fourth Evangelist as one of the three great theologians of the New Testament. In each case we can see the emergence of a distinctively Christian theology in response to the gospel of Jesus Christ. So in Hebrews we see Christian theology in the making, as the writer (to whom I shall refer to as Hebrews) builds up his argument on the meaning of Christ's death. We share in a creative experience because Hebrews has seized ideas not previously exploited.

Two ideas are unique in the New Testament. The priesthood of Jesus after the order of Melchizedek is entirely new, and adds a fresh dimension to the development of christology. There is no evidence that this had been applied to Jesus previously.[1] We shall see that it was wrung from Hebrews by the special needs of the problem to which the letter is addressed. Similarly his use of the ceremonial of the Day of Atonement to expound the sacrificial death of Jesus goes beyond any previous expositions of the faith that 'Christ died for our sins' (1 Cor. 15.3). Again it arises directly from the particular character of the pressing problem which confronts Hebrews.

---

[1] It has been suggested that the idea is mentioned in 2.17 as something that is familiar to the readers. But here it is only a metaphor, which the author uses to prepare the ground for his statement that Jesus really is a high priest in 5.1–10. It has also been argued that 5.1–10 is based on an earlier christological hymn, but this is sheer speculation. The whole passage is thoroughly in the style of Hebrews and requires the context of the larger argument of the epistle.

Hebrews belongs to a creative phase in the early history of Christianity. It is a time when the church is moving into new places and different cultural situations. The simple gospel of the primitive kerygma raises questions not previously posed, and answers have to be found for them. The people addressed in Hebrews cannot be identified with any of the main groups of Christians known to us in the New Testament. They are not Pauline Christians and they are not Johannine Christians, and they do not belong to the mother church in Jerusalem. In Hebrews we have a glimpse into a segment of earliest Christianity unknown from other sources.

Theological argument is prominent in Hebrews, and so it is often held to be a theological treatise. But this is a misleading description, because it is really a practical response to an urgent situation. The readers are on the verge of taking action which Hebrews regards as nothing less than denial of the Christian faith. His object is to persuade them to change their minds and desist from this disastrous course. The theology is the argument which he develops to achieve his object. Hebrews, even more than Romans, is a sustained argument, and the theology is liable to be misrepresented if it is detached from the argument.

This practical purpose explains the rhetorical character of Hebrews. The Greek style of the author is the most accomplished in the New Testament. He has evidently had the benefit of some measure of Greek education, like Paul, and that means some training in the art of rhetoric. In this letter he uses all the resources at his disposal to press home his point. Rhetoric is the art of persuasion, and Hebrews is a work of persuasion from start to finish.

Unfortunately the argument of Hebrews is not easily grasped. Many readers are baffled by it. It is constantly interrupted by digressions and moral exhortations. These sometimes display an appalling rigorism, which has caused misery to readers of a tender conscience all through the centuries. When the main argument is resumed the reader hopes to follow it better, but soon gets lost once more.

A more serious difficulty is that the whole argument has an

alien character from a modern point of view. There are constant quotations from Scripture, but the method of using it is difficult for modern people to appreciate. The preoccupation with the details of ancient laws of sacrifice is liable to make the reader feel out of sympathy with the author. In any case it belongs to a world view which is very different from our own. The connection with the death of Jesus often seems artificial. In general the argument seems to belong to an enclosed world of meaning which is archaic and not immediately accessible to us today.

At the same time every reader is likely to feel the writer's rhetorical power. The opening chapter, with its measured phrases and balanced clauses, describing Jesus as the culmination of the prophetic revelation and raised to the rank of divine Sonship above the angels, is enormously impressive. The recurring contrast between the old sacrifices and the permanent efficacy of the death of Jesus constantly introduces memorable and inspiring statements. The impact of the great 'faith' chapter 11, culminating in the stirring exhortation of 12.1–2, is irresistible. The beautiful blessing at the end, in which Hebrews invokes 'the God of peace, who brought again from the dead our Lord Jesus Christ, the great shepherd of the sheep, by the blood of the eternal covenant' (13.20), is much used in modern liturgies for the blessing of the congregation. These examples at once illustrate the richness of Hebrews in theological ideas and biblical allusions and his capacity to appeal to the emotions of the readers.

The task before us is to seize the distinctive features of the theology of Hebrews and to see how it relates to the theology of the New Testament as a whole and what it has to say to us today. Because of the close connection between the theology and the practical purpose of the letter we shall have to keep the argument constantly in view. This means that we must first try to reconstruct the historical situation which has provoked the writing of this remarkable letter.

THE SITUATION OF THE READERS

The traditional view is that Hebrews is written to a group of Jewish converts who are in danger of relapsing into Judaism. They have lost their original fervour and hanker after the temple worship with its splendid ceremonial and miss the security of the traditions of their Jewish past. The aim of the letter is to persuade them to remain in the church with renewed confidence in the Christian confession of faith.[2]

This view still has its supporters today, and a fresh, and I hope more convincing, version of it is given below and forms the basis of interpretation for our study of the theology of Hebrews. Some of the more recent presentations of it strain credulity by bringing in speculative reconstructions based on supposed links with other parts of the New Testament. Thus Spicq, observing the Jewish Hellenistic character of Hebrews, connects it with the group around Stephen (Acts 6–7). This is fine as far as it goes. But Spicq then suggests that the preoccupation with sacrificial ceremonial points specifically to the 'great crowd of priests' who 'became obedient to the faith' mentioned in the same context (Acts 6.7) as the addressees. He assumes that they are exiled from Jerusalem, and long to return to their old life and to minister once more in the temple. He disregards the fact that Hebrews never once suggests that the readers might themselves have officiated in the temple. In fact Hebrews always refers to the tent, or tabernacle, in the wilderness, as described in Exodus and Leviticus, and what he has to say is theoretical and not related directly to the experience of the readers.[3]

The theory of Montefiore also gets into difficulties because of his identification of the author.[4] Following a suggestion of Luther, he ascribes the letter to Apollos, the Jew from Alexan-

[2] See the careful argument for this position in F. F. Bruce, *The Epistle to the Hebrews*, New London Commentary (London, 1965), pp. xxiii–xxx.

[3] Spicq, *L'Epître aux Hébreux* (2 vols., Paris, 1952, reprinted in Sources bibliques, Paris, 1977), I, pp. 226–31. Spicq later modified this view by assuming that the addressees were drawn from the predominantly priestly Essenes ('L'Epître aux Hébreux: Apollos, Jean-Baptiste, les Hellénistes et Qumran', *RQ*, I (1958–9), 365ff.).

[4] H. W. Montefiore, *Epistle to the Hebrews*, Black's NT Commentaries (London, 1964), pp. 9–29.

dria who was converted at Corinth (Acts 18.24–8; 1 Cor. 1.12; 3.4–6, etc.). He imagines that Apollos is writing to Jewish converts at Corinth, who are under pressure from the local Jews to relapse, but at the same time are deeply opposed to Paul's championship of the Gentiles. It is so difficult to relate Hebrews to what we know of the situation at Corinth from Paul's letters that Montefiore has to date Hebrews to the time before 1 Corinthians was written. It is then difficult to explain what effect it might have had on the situation that Paul actually had to deal with. In any case Hebrews shows no sign of opposition to Paul.

A common feature of these views is the assumption that the readers, if they return to Judaism, would be able to participate in the worship of the temple at Jerusalem, or at least be associated with it by paying the temple tax and by occasional pilgrimages, as was common among Jews of the Dispersion. This requires a date before AD 70, when the temple was destroyed and the sacrificial system ceased. But Hebrews never refers to the temple, as just pointed out, and the theoretical way in which he speaks about the tent and its cultus has suggested that the letter was written after the destruction, perhaps late in the century. It cannot have been written later than 90–95, because it is quoted by Clement of Rome in his letter to the Corinthians, generally dated about 96. Most theories of the later date make little attempt to relate the emphasis on the details of sacrifice to the situation of the readers. Some even think that the readers are Gentile Christians, who have a deep interest in the Jewish Scriptures, and need to understand the Christian gospel in relation to them more accurately.[5] This is then claimed to be part of a general slackness and loss of fervour among the readers, which is the reason for the bracing exhortations which so often interrupt the argument. More will be said about these theories in a later section. They are unsatisfactory, because they cannot account for the urgency and anxiety which characterise the letter from end to end.

A recent exception is the theory of Schmithals, who connects

[5] Notably Moffatt and Windisch; cf. Bruce, p. xxv.

the writing of Hebrews with the growing estrangement between church and synagogue in the period after the fall of Jerusalem, culminating in the exclusion of Gentile Christians (and Jewish Christians too).[6] He argues that this would deprive Christians of the official protection given to Jews by the Romans at the same time as making them endure continuing Jewish hostility. Hebrews thus aims to give them fresh confidence in their isolated and vulnerable situation by showing that their Christian profession fulfils all that they have valued in the scriptural tradition of Judaism and points the way forward to a more perfect following of Christ. The chief problem with this attractive reconstruction is that, though it allows for a hankering after Judaism, return to active association with Judaism is no longer a live option. We thus miss the sense that Hebrews is extremely anxious to dissuade the readers from taking what he regards as a disastrous course of action.

The key to a more satisfactory reconstruction of the situation is provided by careful observation of the rhetorical structure of Hebrews.[7] As the identity of the author and of his readers, the place of writing and the date are all unknown, we are completely dependent on internal evidence. Fortunately a good deal of information can be gleaned from chapter 13.

In the first place it is clear from this chapter that Hebrews is definitely a *letter*. This is often denied, because there is no epistolary opening at the beginning.[8] It is then regarded as a homily or treatise. But the ending (13.22–5) is that of a letter. Some scholars take this concluding section to be an interpolation aimed at bringing Hebrews into line with the tradition of Paul's letters (which would also account for the mention of Timothy in 13.23). But it is already clear from 13.19 that the author writes from a distance. Hence Buchanan even removes

---

[6] See W. Schmithals, *Neues Testament und Gnosis* (Darmstadt, 1984), pp. 138ff., summarised in R. McL. Wilson, *Hebrews*, New Century Bible (Basingstoke and Grand Rapids, 1987), p. 14.

[7] Cf. B. Lindars, 'The Rhetorical Structure of Hebrews', *NTS*, 35 (1989), 382–406.

[8] Cf. J. Swetnam, 'On the Literary Genre of the "Epistle" to the Hebrews', *NovT*, 11 (1969), 261–9.

the whole of chapter 13 as a later addition.[9] But it has far too many links with the body of the letter for this to be plausible. We must conclude that Hebrews is written as an address to be read at the Christian assembly, finishing with the blessing in 13.20–1. It has been written by an amanuensis, but the author has added a final appeal and greetings in his own hand before sending it off. It thus functions as a letter in much the same way as Paul's letter to the Romans. The author himself actually calls it a 'word of exhortation' (13.22). But the point is that Hebrews embodies his address to these people from afar.

Next we should notice that he expresses the anxiety which he feels about the reception of the letter in 13.22 by making an appeal in his own hand. Though the letter has been composed with immense care, he cannot be sure of winning the agreement of the readers. This implies that he is dealing with a most difficult and delicate issue. It is not enough to suppose that all they need is a pep-talk.

Looking further back to verses 18 and 19, we find that the same anxiety is apparent when he asks the readers for their prayers. It is also clear that he is well known to them, though he has to be absent for the time being. In fact it is most natural to assume that he is a member of the same community of Christians. Some commentators think that his enforced absence means imprisonment, but Westcott pointed out that the reference to Timothy in verse 23 implies some freedom of movement.

Before this he charges the readers to 'obey your leaders and submit to them' (verse 17). From this we can deduce that they are not the whole congregation, but a dissident group, such as is implied in 1 John.[10] This illuminates the opening words of the chapter: 'Let brotherly love continue' (13.1). It will become clear, as we become more familiar with Hebrews, that he varies his tone according to the needs of the moment. He knows the value of both understatement and exaggeration. Here the function of the final chapter requires understatement,

---

[9] G. W. Buchanan, *To the Hebrews*, Anchor Bible (Garden City, 1972), pp. 267f.

[10] For the dissident group in 1 John see R. E. Brown, *The Community of the Beloved Disciple* (New York and London, 1979).

because nothing must be done to alienate the readers after they have been subjected to an address of such emotional power. We are thus justified in perceiving a major disruption behind the command to maintain brotherly love. When he says further that the leaders will have to give account of the readers, and might have to do so 'sadly' (verse 17), we should probably think of the coming judgment (Bruce compares Phil. 2.16), which Hebrews asserts is near (10.25). The implication is that the situation is extremely serious, and the leaders are at their wits' end to know how to cope with it.

This then suggests the reason why Hebrews has been brought into the affair. It is because he is a member of the church who is much loved and respected. The leaders have written to him, urging him to intervene in the crisis. Perhaps they hope that he will be able to come in person. This is impossible, however, and so he has responded with this letter. If this is correct, then we can understand why it has been composed with such immense care, using every available device of rhetorical skill to make the most powerful impact on the readers. For this letter is the last resort. If it fails, the leaders have nothing more that they can do to save the situation.

What, then, is the crisis to which the letter is addressed? We can get an idea of it by looking back to 13.7–16. The readers are exhorted to remember their leaders, but this means 'those who spoke to you the word of God'. This, it is generally agreed, refers to the original missionaries who first evangelised them. It is implied that they are not a former generation, unknown to the present members of the church, but people whom they should be able to remember personally. The notable thing about these evangelists is the quality of their life which issued from their faith. Some commentators think that the unusual word for 'outcome' (*ekbasis*) of their life is intended to suggest martyrdom, but it need not do so. But the point is that the exemplary quality of their life was the fruit of the faith which they maintained. We shall see that in Hebrews faith does not mean the content of the Christian confession, i.e. what I believe, but the quality of faithfulness in living in accordance with the Christian confession, i.e. what I do as a believer. Thus the outcome of the life of these evangelists was their life of faith based on the confession. The readers can have the same quality of life if they are equally true to the original confession.

Behind this brief instruction there lies the major issue of the whole letter. The readers are tempted to take a course of action which is inconsistent with the gospel which they originally received. They might be less likely to do so, if they remembered how effective faithfulness to the gospel was in the lives of those who first preached to them. In the following verses, 8–16, Hebrews summarises the practical aspects of this major issue. We must not forget that at this point he has deliberately dropped the severe tone which he has used in the body of the letter, as he does not want to alienate the readers. One feature of what he now has to say is the use of allusive references to matters that are so well known that he does not need to specify them exactly. This makes these verses difficult to interpret, so that there are considerable differences of opinion among modern scholars. But the device is deliberate, as it helps Hebrews to take his readers, who do know what he is talking about, into his confidence, and so increases the rapport which he wants to build up so as to gain acceptance of his whole attempt to make them change their minds. Persuading people to change their minds is always difficult, and especially so when their emotions are strongly engaged in their intended course of action. It can only be done by winning their emotions. Cold logic is not enough.

So first he reminds them of the basis of faith, Jesus Christ, and the point is that this is unchanging, 'the same yesterday and today and for ever' (verse 8). There may be an allusion here to the most primitive form of the confession of faith, 'Jesus is the Christ.'[11] This is in fact the point from which the whole letter started (1.1–4). Hebrews had taken care to begin the letter with a statement of faith which he knew the readers

[11] 'Jesus Christ' would not be the primitive confession as such, which would be *Christos Iēsous* (= Jesus is the Christ); see V. Neufeld, *The Earliest Christian Confessions* (Leiden, 1963), pp. 140–6.

shared, because it was just as important to begin in a way that would be likely to gain their goodwill as to finish in this way.

The next words warn against 'strange teachings' and unprofitable 'foods' (verse 9). What is meant has to be deduced from the substance of the whole of the letter. We are helped by the contrast in verse 10, where Hebrews claims that 'we have an altar from which those who serve the tent have no right to eat'. Those who serve the tent are clearly the Levitical priests, as described in chapter 9. This suggests that the strange teachings are the details of atonement sacrifice which were there set out. If so, the whole point at issue is a felt need on the part of the readers to resort to Jewish customs in order to come to terms with their sense of sin against God and need for atonement. Thus the central argument of the letter is precisely a compelling case for the complete and abiding efficacy of Jesus' death as an atoning sacrifice. What, then, are the 'foods, which have not benefited their adherents'?[12] We can think of the sacrificial meals in the temple. But if, as seems more likely, the readers are far away in the Dispersion, the reference is probably to synagogue meals, held especially at festival times to give the worshippers a stronger sense of solidarity with the worship of the temple in Jerusalem. This of course does not mean meals directly associated with atonement sacrifices, but meals which strengthen the sense of solidarity with the temple where the whole sacrificial system, with its daily offerings, is performed on behalf of Jews everywhere.[13]

[12] Some scholars argue that the reference is to the Christian eucharist, which Hebrews disapproves. If so, the 'strange teachings' must be some Christian teaching which he regards as heretical. It also follows that the Christian assembly referred to in verses 10–15 is non-eucharistic, as Hebrews is on this view an anti-sacramentalist. With regard to the latter point it must be said that it depends entirely on the words in verse 9, and if that is not a reference to the eucharist there is nothing to show whether the assembly was eucharistic or not. The important point is that it was an occasion when 'the Lord's death is proclaimed', as in the eucharistic description of 1 Cor. 11.26. With regard to the 'strange teachings' it really is most strange that Hebrews should bring in a new topic at this very late stage in his letter without making it clear what the teachings are. My interpretation has the merit of taking these verses closely with the letter as a whole. For the debate on these verses see especially the commentaries of Bruce and Wilson.

[13] For Jewish life in the Diaspora see E. Schürer, *The History of the Jewish People in the Age of Jesus Christ*, revised edition (3 vols., Edinburgh, 1973–87), III.i, pp. 138–49.

The reason why these meals are referred to at this point (and not previously mentioned in the main agrument) is that the idea opens up the contrast which follows in verse 10. Christians have their own 'altar', i.e. the sacrifice of Christ (naturally Hebrews does not mean the altar in church, as older commentators often assumed, as the word was not applied to the communion table as early as this). The sacrifice of Christ is proclaimed in every meeting of Christians for worship, especially in the eucharist (cf. 1 Cor 11.26). The readers then should not be frequenting synagogue worship in order to feel the benefit of the sacrificial system (which is any case illusory, verse 9), but should gladly participate in the Christian worship in which the sacrifice of Christ is celebrated.

Hebrews is well aware that this means breaking the relationship which his readers have formed with the local Jewish community. This may be difficult emotionally because it was meeting their need, or at least they thought it would do so. If they have received kindly encouragement from their Jewish neighbours, that would make it even more difficult, especially as (being born Jews themselves) they are their friends and relations. As it seems that the two communities were normally estranged, seeing that Hebrews regards this return to Judaism as virtual apostasy (6.6), it is likely to renew old bitterness and hostility if the readers now break away again from the Jews (compare verse 13 with 10.32–4). So Hebrews must show that he understands the dilemma and encourage them to make the break all the same. But at this stage in the letter he has to do it gently and positively, so as to help them to feel able to accept his demand. He therefore takes up another facet of the sacrificial ceremonial which he has not previously mentioned, the burning of the bodies of the animals 'outside the camp' (verse 11). This has a counterpart in Jesus' crucifixion 'outside the gate' (verse 12) and suggests the model for Christians (verse 13). It does of course mean facing suffering, but in any case the time is short and the reward is sure (verse 14). So they should spend their time singing the praise of Jesus in company with their fellow Christians (verse 15, probably referring once more to the eucharistic assembly), and also undertake works of mercy, which are as acceptable to God as a sacrifice (verse 16).

The emphasis on participation in the Christian assembly is an important matter in view of Hebrews' complaint that some (and therefore not the whole of the dissident group) have been tending to stay away from it (10.25). It is thus implied that they were tending to feel greater benefit from the synagogue meetings, and had lost confidence in the value of the Christian assembly. The particular reason for this is the problem of their consciousness of sin (9.9, 14; 10.2). This is why we must see the argument of Hebrews as pre-eminently practical. It is aimed at persuading the readers that recourse to the Jewish community is the wrong way to go about it. On the contrary the right thing to do is to take part in the Christian assembly, in which the wholly sufficient sacrifice of Christ is celebrated, and do practical good works, which Christians and Jews alike regard as having some atoning value (cf. Tobit 12.9). It is of course necessary to bear in mind that there is nothing to do with Paul's contrast between faith and works in Hebrews, so that there was no reason to question this commonly accepted view. For Hebrews it helps to give his readers the sense of something practical that they can do. This reflects the first part of the chapter (13.1–6), in which he gives general practical suggestions in maintaining the life of faith. He mentions these first so as to set the tone of this concluding chapter in a non-controversial way. They are basic moral matters which show that Christianity embraces the whole of life.

One more crucial question remains to be faced. Why is it that the readers have lost confidence in the power of the sacrifice of Christ to deal with their consciousness of sin? If the above reconstruction of the situation is correct, this must be seen as the root issue. It is the reason why these people have got themselves into such an unhappy position, unable to accept the assurances of their fellow Christians and turning to the Jewish community from which they had previously separated themselves, thereby causing friction and division in the church and presenting the leaders with a problem which they cannot resolve. Can we find any comparable situation in the

New Testament which may help us to understand their dilemma?

There is in fact a comparable problem in the case of the Thessalonians. It appears from 1 Thess. 4.13 that, since the converts enthusiastically accepted Paul's preaching and 'turned to God from idols, to serve a living and true God, and to wait for his Son from heaven, whom he raised from the dead, Jesus who delivers us from the wrath to come' (1 Thess. 1.9–10), some of their number have died. Because Paul had given the impression that the time of waiting would be very short, no one had asked what would happen to any who might die first. Evidently Paul himself had not felt any necessity to allow for it in his teaching. This can scarcely be due to the novelty of the situation, as it is not to be supposed that no one in the Christian communities had died during his years as a missionary. It is more likely that he took it for granted that the converts would know how to adjust their understanding of the gospel to cope with such an eventuality. So their evident distress and confusion have taken him by surprise. He replies by giving further detail about the message which he had originally proclaimed (1 Thess. 4.13–5.11).

This is surely very similar to the underlying problem of Hebrews' readers. They received the gospel of Jesus Christ (2.3–4; 13.7–8), and that must certainly have included the basic kerygma that 'Christ died for our sins' (1 Cor. 15.3). But this was presented as complete atonement for past sins. Their baptism gave assurance of forgiveness of the sins of their former life.[14] But nothing was said about post-baptismal sin. They simply assumed that they would remain in a state of grace until the parousia. But as time passed, some of them at least began to be oppressed by renewed consciousness of sin, and the gospel as they had received it appeared not to allow for it. We can imagine that the leaders took a pastoral concern (verse 17), and tried hard to persuade them that Christ's sacrifice covers the present as well as the past. But if we may judge from Rev. 5.9–10 and similar passages, the Christian

---

[14] For the practice of baptism in the Hebrews church see below, pp. 67, 103–4.

liturgy did not make this plain.[15] On the other hand they knew from their Jewish past that atonement for sin is constantly attended to in Jewish liturgy. The return to the Jewish community thus offered a practical way of coping with a problem which was deeply felt and not adequately provided for in the Christian teaching which they had received.

From a practical point of view what the readers need is renewed confidence in the value of the Christian liturgy. This is why Hebrews mentions it in 13.10–16 as the alternative to Jewish practices. But they will regain confidence only if they can be convinced that it can meet their present need. This involves two things.

In the first place they must be shown, in a way that the leaders have so far failed to achieve, that the sacrificial death of Jesus, though an event in the past, has continuing efficacy. This must be done not in an abstract way but in relation to the Jewish theory and practice of atonement which the readers themselves accept. This explains why Hebrews uses the ceremonies of the Day of Atonement in his central argument. It provides an agreed standard and basis for his purpose. At the same time it is not merely a matter of repetition of a case which the readers have heard before. It is a highly original line of argument tailored specifically for their needs. It makes the essential point (which is most important for our study of the theology of Hebrews) that the death of Jesus is not merely a sacrifice for sins, as is stated in the kerygma, but has ongoing effect for all time. We shall see how skilfully he achieves this object in the body of the letter.

The second point is that it is not sufficient to leave the matter at the level of theory. The readers have a real and distressing problem of conscience. They need to *feel* that they are forgiven. So part of the argument is devoted to explaining how their knowledge of atonement can be experienced in the present and maintained in the future. The final part of the main argument on the sacrifice of Jesus (10.1–18) deals with this question as far as the present is concerned. But with regard to the future,

[15] For early pre-Pauline formulae of the atoning death of Jesus and its meaning in the primitive community see M. Hengel, *The Atonement* (London, 1981), pp. 33–75.

Hebrews introduces his concept of faith. The great practical importance which he attaches to it can be seen from the fact that his treatment of it stretches from 10.19 to 12.29, and comprises some of his most powerful rhetoric, including the great chapter on faith. He thus aims to inspire them so strongly that they can have the emotional pull to make the decision to abandon their present intentions and participate in the liturgy and life of the Christian community with their consciences clear and with renewed confidence and zeal. From this point of view the section on faith can be seen to be an essential and indispensable part of the total argument. Without it the object of Hebrews could not be achieved. It is thus not a kind of optional extra after the argument is over, as is so often assumed. Finally the blessing in 13.20–1 picks up what is said here, thus confirming it as Hebrews' parting thought to his readers. The reference to 'the blood of the eternal covenant' in verse 20 refers to the whole central argument, which concludes with the covenant in 10.16, and the rest of the blessing relates to the life of faith which Hebrews hopes the readers will lead as a result of his stirring address to them.

The above reconstruction of the situation of the readers has been based entirely on an integrated reading of chapter 13, interpreted in the light of hints elsewhere in the letter. It has given some idea of the aim and importance of the theology of Hebrews. It has also drawn attention to factors that must constantly be borne in mind as we consider the theology of Hebrews in detail. These are the essentially practical purpose of the argument and the rhetorical character of the whole composition.

PERSONS, PLACES, AND DATE

Some further words must be said on these subjects briefly, because they have a bearing on the interpretation of Hebrews.

First, the *author* has been traditionally identified with Paul. If this were correct it would obviously have a very important effect on our assessment of Hebrews, as has just been pointed out in connection with faith and good works. However, it is clear that the attribution of the letter to Paul (first by Clement of Alexandria in the late second century[16]) was promoted to gain acceptance of it in the canon of the New Testament at a time when there was much dispute about which books should be included. Clement argued that the style was different from the rest of Paul's letters because he wrote this one in Hebrew and someone else (Luke) translated it – an impossible view in the light of 10.5–10, where the argument depends on the Greek (Septuagint) version of the Psalms.[17] He also suggested that Paul omitted the usual epistolary opening giving his name, because it would be too dangerous on account of the Judaistic controversy. But it is clear that the real author was unknown. Clement of Rome, writing to Corinth about AD 96, knows Paul's letters, but quotes from Hebrews without any indication that it might be by Paul.[18] Tertullian, writing about AD 220, attributes it to Barnabas, Paul's fellow apostle.[19] But this is because he saw a similarity in the handling of Scripture to the spurious *Epistle of Barnabas*, which is an extravagantly anti-Jewish tract. We shall have to consider the use of Scripture in Hebrews later.

The question of authorship was raised at the Reformation by Luther, who had good reason to doubt the traditional ascription to Paul, and attributed it to Apollos on account of the Alexandrian character of the thought of Hebrews (cf. Acts 18.24).[20] This draws attention to the influences behind the thought of Hebrews, which we shall also have to take into

---

[16] Clement's opinion is quoted in Euseb., *H.E.* VI.14.3–4. The oldest known manuscript of the Pauline Letters (P[46], c. AD 200) belongs to the same time, and includes Hebrews directly after Romans. The majority of manuscripts, however, place it in the familiar position at the end of the Paulines, thus reflecting the uncertainty about the authorship.

[17] Ps. 40.6–8, where the word 'body', which is essential to Hebrews' argument, is a mistranslation of the Hebrew 'ear'. So also the argument in 9.15–17 depends on the range of meanings of Greek *diathēkē*.

[18] The only extensive quotation is 1 *Clem.* 36.1–5, which is an abbreviated version of Heb. 1.1–13. Quotations of Num. 12.7 in 1 *Clem.* 17.5; 43.1 may allude to Heb. 3.5.

[19] Tertullian, *On Modesty* 20.

[20] Luther originally assumed that the author was Paul, but his change of view becomes apparent in his *Preface to Hebrews* (1522), and he definitely ascribes Hebrews to Apollos in a sermon of 1537 and in his *Commentary on Genesis* of 1545 (see Bruce, p. xxxix, n. 72 for references).

account. Calvin thought that the author might be Luke because of the very good Greek style, or possibly Clement of Rome himself.[21]

Numerous other suggestions have been made in modern scholarship, but commentators are increasingly reluctant to identify the author with any individual named in the New Testament (so Westcott, W. Manson, Bruce, Wilson and many others). This avoids fruitless speculation and allows proper recognition of the unique character of Hebrews. Nothing can be built on the mention of Timothy in 13.23, though the possibility that he is the same as Paul's companion cannot be excluded. But evidently he is known personally to Hebrews and his readers.

The *address* 'to the Hebrews' remains an unsolved problem.[22] It is most likely that it means a group of Christians who are Jews by race (cf. 2 Cor. 11.22; Phil. 3.5). A less probable suggestion is that it means Gentile Christians who are imbued with Jewish spirituality before their conversion. The designation is ancient, being found in the oldest manuscript of the Pauline letters, which includes Hebrews (P[46], c. AD 200), and known to Clement of Alexandria. But it may be only a deduction from the contents of the letter to provide a convenient designation for reference. In any case it gives no idea of the location.

A connection with Rome is suggested by several factors. People from Italy are mentioned in 13.24, but we do not know how they relate to the readers. They may be members of the readers' own group, in which case the readers live in Italy, possibly in Rome (though one would expect Rome to be mentioned explicitly if this is the case). Alternatively they may be the people among whom the author is staying who join him in sending greetings from Italy. Or they could be a group from Italy known to both the author and the readers who happen to be where the author is staying (Montefiore thinks of Priscilla

---

[21] J. Calvin, *Commentary on Hebrews* (1549) on Heb. 13.23.

[22] In Acts 6.1 'Hebrews' means Aramaic-speaking Jews as opposed to Hellenists (Greek-speaking Jews), a usage which is also found in Philo. This cannot be the meaning here if Hebrews was composed in Greek as maintained above. For discussion of the problems see Bruce, pp. xxiiif.

and Aquila). Rome had a 'synagogue of the Hebrews', but that just means a Jewish meeting-place, and tells us nothing. More weight attaches to the fact that Hebrews was known in Rome to Clement of Rome at an early date, but was not falsely attributed to Paul there until much later.

Rome is favoured as the destination by a number of scholars, but it is not without difficulties.[23] If we are right in thinking that the readers are Jewish Christians, they can scarcely be the same group as the mixed, but predominantly Gentile, congregation presupposed in Romans. In any event the situation is entirely different. However, it is not impossible that there are several independent Christian groups in Rome, which had at least eleven Jewish synagogues. The congregations tended to be separate because of the Roman laws prohibiting large associations. But two events in Rome would be likely to leave a mark on Hebrews, if it were sent to Rome. One is the expulsion of Jews from Rome by the emperor Claudius in AD 49 (Acts 18.2), which was not revoked until the accession of Nero in 54. The other is the persecution of Christians following the great fire of Rome (which Nero blamed on the Christians) in 64. We hear of sufferings among the Hebrews Christians in the early days after their conversion (10.32–4), but these might have been due to breaking away from the Jewish community rather than state persecution or mob violence. The Neronian persecution seems to be excluded by 12.4, though the verse could refer to this as a dire warning, if the letter was sent elsewhere at about this time.

Other possibilities tend to be connected with theories of authorship (for instance Montefiore's proposal of Corinth) or with characteristic features of Hebrews.[24] Thus the concentration on sacrifice has suggested Jerusalem (Wm Ramsay, C. H. Turner), but the consistent reference to the tent in the wilderness rather than the temple makes this unlikely. Alexandria (C. J. Cadoux, S. G. F. Brandon and others) suits the thought

[23] This is strongly argued by William Manson, *The Epistle to the Hebrews*, Baird Lecture, 1949 (London, 1951), and taken up more cautiously by Bruce.
[24] For these and many other suggestions see Bruce, pp. xxxi–xxxv; Spicq, I, pp. 220–52.

of Hebrews, as we shall see, but it is really excluded by the fact that it was in Alexandria that it was first attributed to Paul. The best that can be said is that nothing forbids the view that Hebrews is addressed to comparatively well-educated Jewish Christians somewhere in the Mediterranean Dispersion.

For the *date* of Hebrews we can see a steady movement away from the traditional position, which presupposed that the temple was still in operation, to a rather later date among more recent scholars.[25] This, as already explained above, cannot be later than AD 96, the date usually assigned to 1 *Clement*. There are two main factors here, both relevant to a proper appreciation of the theology of Hebrews.

There is first the question whether Hebrews presupposes that the temple service is operative or not. Why are the references to sacrifice always biblical, quoting or alluding to Exodus and Leviticus, speaking of the tent and never referring to the existing temple? The answer seems obvious that it is because the temple no longer exists and its cultus has come to an end. If so, Hebrews must have been written later than AD 70.[26] However, the theology of Hebrews points to a different explanation. If the readers are resorting to Judaism to cope with their consciousness of sin, as suggested in my reconstruction above, they will be persuaded that the sacrifice of Jesus is sufficient only if it can be shown that it meets their own understanding of what is required to make atonement. Now the proper standard is provided by the Law, which in their view is the revealed will of God. So Hebrews bases his argument on the directions for the Day of Atonement, choosing this ceremony deliberately, because its importance in Jewish life gives it pre-eminence among all biblical references to

---

[25] Proponents of a late date (usually c. AD 85) include R. H. Fuller (*A Critical Introduction to the New Testament* (London, 1966), p. 147), W. G. Kümmel (*Introduction to the New Testament* (London, 1975), p. 304), H. Koester (*Introduction to the New Testament* (Philadelphia, 1982), II, p. 272), and Schmithals (n. 6 above). Wilson, p. 14, is reluctant to accept this majority view, and favours a date in the late sixties as argued by J. A. T. Robinson (*Redating the New Testament* (London, 1976), pp. 200–20).

[26] Hebrews has actually been used as evidence for the continuation of sacrifices on the ruined site of the temple after AD 70, but it seems certain that sacrifices really did cease: see Schürer (n. 13 above), I, pp. 521–3.

atonement. Hebrews simply presupposes that what is done in the temple (or used to be done, if it is destroyed) accords with the standard of the Law.

This means that we cannot use this factor to decide the date of Hebrews. It has been pointed out that 1 *Clement* 40–1 speaks of the Levitical priesthood without giving any sign that the priestly functions have ceased. But other factors need to be taken into account. Firstly Hebrews gives no impression that the readers were turning to a spiritualising of sacrifice which was considered more effective than the spirituality of the sacrifice of the death of Jesus. It is always presupposed that the actual sacrificial system is the only alternative on offer. This does not mean that the readers would have to be within range of the temple, only that they would wish to have the practical means of feeling solidarity with its worship which were open to all Diaspora Jews. It is known, however, that wealthy Diaspora Jews in New Testament times came to live in Jerusalem so as to take an active part in the worship of the temple. Secondly the repeated emphasis on the fact that the sacrificial system is obsolescent makes it almost inconceivable that Hebrews should not mention the destruction of the temple, if that had already taken place. These two factors gain considerable force when it is conceded that Hebrews writes to a real and urgent situation and when the rhetorical character of the letter is given full recognition. Thus on balance a date before AD 70 seems to be required.

The other main factor for dating Hebrews is the claim that the theology is characteristic of second-generation Christianity (often misleadingly, but conveniently, referred to as early catholicism). It is best represented in the Pastoral Epistles. It is marked by an advanced christology, in which Jesus tends to be spoken of as God, by loss of immediate expectation of the parousia (second coming of Jesus), by care for the deposit of faith as a body of doctrine, by increasing emphasis on the institutional aspects of the church in ministry and sacraments, and by warnings against heresy which actually illustrate the fact that extraneous teaching is more and more creeping into the church.

On all these counts the accusation against Hebrews fails. As will be shown later, the christology of Hebrews does not go beyond what is found in Col. 1.15–20, which is generally dated to AD 65–70 (except by those who claim Paul's authorship of Colossians, which would make it much earlier). Hebrews gives no sense of the fading of the parousia expectation, rather the reverse (10.25, 37). The appeal to the teaching of the founders in 13.7 is not due to loss of vitality, but to the danger of apostasy in the readers' present position, and the whole argument of the letter is directed to dealing with this urgent situation. The concern for the original teaching is no different from that of Paul in 1 Corinthians 1–3. The references to baptism (6.2, disputed because the word is plural, RSV 'ablutions') and to the Christian assembly, possibly meaning the eucharist, in 13.10–16 are also comparable to 1 Corinthians. The designation 'leaders' in 13.7, 17 is not a technical term for Christian ministers like bishops, presbyters and deacons in the Pastoral Epistles and Apostolic Fathers. If our reconstruction of the situation is correct, there is no question of heresy in the sense of new and extraneous doctrine, because the point at issue is the validity of the Jewish teaching which the readers ought to have left behind. The suggestion that either Hebrews or his readers have been influenced by incipient Gnosticism will be considered in the next section. Otherwise it is clear that these considerations do not compel a date later than AD 65–70.

BACKGROUND OF THOUGHT

The Greek language and style of Hebrews are the best in the New Testament and indicate some degree of Greek education, especially in the art of rhetoric. All the Old Testament quotations follow the Septuagint. Though some Semitisms in the language of Hebrews have been claimed, these are mostly due to the influence of the Septuagint, and are certainly not enough to warrant any theory of a Hebrew or Aramaic original. The value of his rhetorical training is constantly evident. Spicq has listed numerous literary devices such as attention to rhythm, chiasmus construction (for example 5.1–10), inclusion (for example 'suffering', 2.10 and 18, frames the paragraph) and anaphora (the repetition of 'by faith' in chapter 11 for cumulative effect).[27] But these merely illustrate the rhetorical skill which has gone into the whole composition so as to achieve the object of persuading the readers to change their minds.

These features naturally suggest an Alexandrian background of thought, because many Jews there were well educated in Greek culture and the need for the Septuagint first arose there, as they no longer spoke Hebrew. Moreover Hebrews alludes to books that were composed in Greek probably in Egypt: for instance 1.3 almost quotes Wisd. 7.25–6, and 11.25 is dependent on 2 Maccabees 6–7. These literary influences do not necessitate locating Hebrews in Alexandria, because the books were well diffused among Greek-speaking Jews. They represent the meeting of Jewish and Greek culture, in which Jews, remaining faithful to their religious traditions, absorbed some of the philosophical interests and moral thought of the Greeks.

This general affiliation to Hellenistic Judaism does not exclude a home in Jerusalem, where Greek language and philosophy had long been a feature of the upper classes.[28] It seems probable that the church of Hebrews ultimately stems from the Hellenistic Jews mentioned in Acts 6–7, as the group of converts fled after the death of Stephen and 'went about preaching the word' (Acts 8.4). The Hebrews church may well be one of the fruits of this missionary activity. As the charge against Stephen is said to have been opposition to 'this holy place [i.e. the temple] and the law' (Acts 6.13), we can see there the basis of Hebrews' main contention that the atoning sacrifices of the Law have been superseded by the sacrifice of Christ. According to my reconstruction this was seen by Hebrews, in line with the original missionaries (13.7), to entail complete separation from their former Jewish life. The Hebrews Christians thus differ from the Jerusalem church

[27] For fuller details see Spicq, I, pp. 351–70.
[28] See M. Hengel, *Judaism and Hellenism* (2 vols., London, 1974), I, pp. 58–106.

under James, which retained its Jewish life and links, and from Paul, who tried to keep the lines of communication with the Jews open at the same time as evangelising the Gentiles.

The influence of Palestinian Judaism, as distinct from the Alexandrian Judaism represented by the Wisdom of Solomon, is evident in Hebrews' presupposition of God's predetermined plan of salvation culminating in the parousia, which is expected imminently. This also lies behind his concept of the function of the prophetic Scriptures. They witness to the hidden plan of God, which has now been unfolded. These are, of course, positions common to the primitive kerygma. A similar approach to Scripture in relation to the predetermined plan of God is characteristic of the Dead Sea Scrolls. In particular the emphasis on the theme of the priestly Messiah and the use of the character of Melchizedek have been used to claim direct connection with the Qumran Sect, or with the similar Essene sect of the Therapeutae in Egypt. But the handling of both these themes in Hebrews bears no relation to the Qumran documents, as will be shown later. Recent scholarship refuses to see any real connection with Qumran.[29]

The Alexandrian style of Hebrews has also suggested to many scholars the possibility of the influence of Philo (20 BC–AD 50), the wealthy and highly educated Jew of Alexandria, who attempted to make a synthesis of Jewish religious tradition and Greek philosophical thought.[30] There are certainly some superficial similarities. Thus Philo held a Platonic idea of reality, in which the unseen, eternal forms of things alone are real, and the created order is a material copy, marked by decay and death. The contrast between the earthly tent and the heavenly reality (Heb. 8.5, quoting Exod. 25.40) and the Law

---

[29] Spicq (article in n. 3 above), H. Kosmala (*Hebräer-Essener-Christen* (Leiden, 1959)) and others argued for the Essene origin of the readers (not even fully converted according to Kosmala). H. Braun supported the idea of close links with Qumran in an article in 1955 (*RB*, 62 (1955), 5ff.), but subsequently revised his opinion (*Qumran und das Neue Testament* (2 vols., Tübingen, 1966)). This followed the criticisms of J. Coppens in 'Les Affinités qumraniennes de l'épître aux Hébreux', *NRT*, 84 (1962), 128–41, 257–82.

[30] For a brief comparison between Philo and Hebrews see Montefiore, pp. 6–9. The standard treatment is R. Williamson, *Philo and the Epistle to the Hebrews* (Leiden, 1970).

as a 'shadow of the good things to come' (10.1) can be taken to support a similar view on the part of Hebrews. But in fact he is thinking of the plan of God and its eschatological fulfilment. The same applies to the interpretation of Scripture. Philo regarded the real meaning of Scripture as purely spiritual, and so treated it, and indeed all the paraphernalia of Jewish worship, allegorically. When Hebrews allegorises the story of Melchizedek (7.1–3), it might be thought that he is following Philo's method. But this is not so, because Hebrews does not deny the historical process. He thinks of the saving act of God in Christ as the decisive event which starts the new era of everlasting life, the transition from the era of the old covenant to the new. He does not deny the literal meaning of the Scriptures, but holds that its direct application has been superseded as a result of this transition. The spiritual meaning of Scripture is its prophetic quality in relation to the plan of God and its fulfilment. Thus, in spite of first impressions, it turns out that Hebrews does not argue on the basis of a Platonised world view at all. Moreover, the exhaustive study of R. Williamson has shown conclusively that Hebrews owes no direct debt to Philo.

Finally the influence of Gnostic ideas must be regarded as theoretically possible because what is known of the second-century Gnostic sects suggests that they began as Platonising theosophical groups directly influenced by Judaism. They thus belong to the fringe of Diaspora Judaism, and one such group could easily have come in contact with the Hebrews church. They reflect Philo's spiritualising outlook and mystical interest, and indeed Philo is in some ways a precursor of Gnostic thought. Käsemann claimed that Hebrews actually aimed to promote a Gnostic interpretation of Christianity, assuming that the contrast between the old sacrifices and Christ is intended to teach a purely spiritual religion with no material elements (cf. 13.15).[31] He thought the leading idea is the pilgrim people of God as presented in chapters 3 and 4, but saw this in terms of Gnostic ideas of the journey of the soul. Koester

---

[31] E. Käsemann, *Das wandernde Gottesvolk* (Göttingen, 1958, repr., 1961); ET *The Wandering People of God* (Minneapolis, 1984).

also regarded this as a Gnostic trait in Hebrews, but he realised that the insistence on the human sufferings and death of Jesus (2.10–18) and the apocalyptic view of the future judgment (10.27) show a firm basis in the primitive Christian tradition and are incompatible with Gnosticism. So he suggested that Hebrews, while showing some influence of Gnostic thought, is actively opposing the Gnostic views held by the readers, who deny the salvatory significance of Jesus' death.[32] But as Wilson has pointed out, the fact that Hebrews and Gnosticism have some phrases and ideas in common does not necessarily require any historical link. It is much more to the point that all the decisive features, such as creation by the Demiurge and the world as a prison of the soul, are entirely absent from Hebrews.[33]

It remains to be said that the chief influence on the thought of Hebrews is the mainstream of Christian life and teaching. Hebrews not only appeals to the first missionaries but also builds on the chief items of the primitive kerygma. The new features do not mark departure from the tradition. They are rather explications of it. Hebrews shows some influence from the characteristics of Hellenistic Judaism, but there is no sign of more radical ideas imported from an extraneous religious system. It is in his handling of the tradition in relation to the crisis facing him that he emerges as one of the three great theologians of the New Testament.

[32] Koester, *Introduction*, II, pp. 272–6.

[33] Wilson, pp. 25–7. Mention may also be made of the theory of M. Rissi, *Die Theologie des Hebräerbriefs* (Tübingen, 1987), that the readers are cultivating a mystical sense of direct access to God, comparable to the spirituality of some of the Qumran texts, and disregard the need for atonement for sin. This view fails to observe the rhetorical skill with which Hebrews repeatedly seeks to reassure the readers of the pastoral concern of Jesus as high priest (e.g. 2.17–18; 4.14–16), which implies that the readers are deeply troubled by the sense of sin.

CHAPTER 2

The Theology of Hebrews

THE FOUNDATION IN THE PRIMITIVE KERYGMA

Hebrews is notable for its highly skilled composition and powerful rhetorical effect. We have seen that recognition of the rhetorical character of Hebrews is fundamental for a true understanding of the letter. It has been carefully composed to persuade the readers to abandon their wish to return to the Jewish community in order to heal their troubled consciences, and to renew their confidence that healing is to be found in the gospel and its expression in Christian life.

The theology of Hebrews is the argument used to achieve this aim. Hebrews is not an abstract theological treatise, but thoroughly practical in intention. It is a mistake to look for a leading idea as the key to the whole (for instance Nairne suggested that Hebrews enunciates what he called the sacramental principle).[1] Nor will it do to regard Hebrews as a 'midrash' on Psalm 110 (Buchanan), which suggests a doubtful use of 'midrash' (which properly denotes the exposition of the biblical text) and produces a wrong assessment of the place of Psalm 110 in the argument.[2]

Similarly it is unwise to subordinate the theology to the artistic structure. Hebrews is beautifully balanced, but that is not for the sake of giving aesthetic pleasure, but to make the point most effectively. The best-known composition analysis is that of Vanhoye, who found what he regarded as a perfect chiastic structure with its pivot in the centre at 8.1–9.28 on the

---

[1] A. Nairne, *The Epistle of Priesthood* (Edinburgh, 1913), pp. 32–59 and *passim*.
[2] Buchanan, *Hebrews*, pp. xix-xxii.

sacrifice of Christ.[3] This ought then to be the climax of the argument. But apart from the fact that the chiasmus is by no means perfect, because the correspondences are not exact on either side of this central section, the real climax from a rhetorical point of view comes at the conclusion of chapter 12 with its overwhelmingly impressive appeal to the readers. There have been previous climaxes like peaks on the path up the mountain, but the argument runs continuously through the whole letter. But Hebrews does use the literary device of inclusion to bring the thought back to the beginning (for example Jesus as the 'pioneer' in 2.10 and 12.2), which is a well-known method of helping an audience to grasp the argument as a whole.

This point can be of help to our study of the theology of Hebrews, because it enables us to distinguish the innovations from the positions which can be taken as agreed by both author and readers. Hebrews proceeds from the known to the unknown and back to the known at the end. The solemn periodic sentence structure of chapter 1 is aimed at establishing rapport with the readers before winding up to the main issue. The last chapter winds down gently so as to leave the rapport undamaged by the stern message in between. The theme of faith acts as the transition to the main issue in chapter 3 and also moves the argument to its climax in 10.19–12.29 in preparation for the conclusion. These subtle relations of form and content suggest that there is a deeper relationship between chapters 1 and 13 than is generally realised. Chapter 1 is a statement of basic christology in accordance with the teaching of the founders' message of Jesus Christ (13.7–8). As the same theme continues through chapter 2, we should expect to find the previously known and agreed teaching in these two chapters.

This point is confirmed by the rhetorical touches in these two chapters. Chapter 1 refrains altogether from direct address to the readers. It contains only the slightest hint of the real issue which will be tackled, as we shall see in a moment. The beautifully measured opening verses are designed to sound

[3] A. Vanhoye, *La Structure littéraire de l'Epître aux Hébreux* (Paris and Bruges, 1963).

impressive and to set the tone, a deeply serious tone, of what is to follow without any reference to matters of controversy. It is calculated to induce the readers to listen attentively to what is to be said without feeling threatened. It also sets the scale of the composition by making a quite lengthy introduction.

The first intimation that not all is well is given at 2.1. It is done very gently. It is merely suggested that the readers might have relaxed their vigilance and be in danger of 'drifting away' from the original teaching (2.1).[4] The real seriousness of their behaviour is not yet indicated. But Hebrews makes it clear that there could be dire consequences if they neglect the original teaching. This point is made all the more emphatically by reminding them of the impressiveness of the occasion when they received the gospel. The teaching originated from Jesus himself (2.3). It was passed on by those who had actually heard him. Whether this means that these missionaries had heard him or that they continued the succession of those who heard him is disputed, but undoubtedly Hebrews wishes to stress the foundation of what he has to say in the primitive kerygma. He underlines it further by reminding the readers of the 'signs and wonders' and 'gifts of the Holy Spirit' which accompanied their conversion, quite in the manner of Acts (for example Acts 2.43) and Paul (Rom. 15.19). We shall also notice the skill with which he relates the facts of the kerygma to the present need of the readers in what follows. For in drawing attention to the humanity of Jesus he shows how this places him alongside our own human weakness: 'For because he himself has suffered and been tempted, he is able to help those who are tempted' (2.18). Temptation! With their consciousness of sin, that is precisely the readers' problem. So Jesus, the Jesus of the primitive kerygma, is presented as the answer to their need before the real seriousness of their present behaviour has been exposed. Hebrews is determined that it should be clear that his intention is primarily to be helpful.

---

[4] Many commentators have been misled by this verse into supposing that this is the problem facing Hebrews. On this view the letter is a bracing exhortation to buck up and show more convinced and committed discipleship. This completely fails to account for the real urgency of the letter, and illustrates the peril of neglecting the rhetorical structure.

We are thus justified in expecting to find the basic theology of Hebrews in these two chapters, and in seeing in it a close relation to the primitive kerygma. Even if it contains some elements which cannot be regarded as primitive, it is what Hebrews considers to be the original message. The subjects alluded to are the pre-existence of Jesus, his exaltation as Messiah and Son of God, his relation to the angels, his humanity, and his saving death. We shall also see that Hebrews prepares the ground for the subsequent argument by giving gentle hints of themes which will be developed later. In this way the new elements in his theology arise naturally from what has already been given.

The pre-existence of Jesus

The opening statement consists of solemn and balanced clauses, which say a great deal about Jesus, but at the same time leave some things to be taken for granted. Thus the very name of Jesus does not appear at all until we reach 2.9. Before that he is referred to only as the Son (1.2, 8) or the first-born (1.6). This allusive way of writing is not intended to obscure the issues, for there is no real doubt what is meant. It is another example of a feature which we have observed in chapter 13. It helps Hebrews to establish rapport with his readers by taking for granted things that are certainly held in common. He just mentions the points which are fundamental to his theology and must be presupposed in the development of the main argument which will follow.

So he starts with God, and his first point is that God has spoken. There is no definition of God. No philosophical or speculative ideas about God are introduced. The Jewish understanding of God is one of the things that is taken for granted.

What Hebrews does say, however, is of such fundamental importance that it is necessary to consider the opening verses, 1.1–4, in detail. As we shall note the chiasmus construction in these verses, it will be helpful to set them out in verse lines.

¹In many and various ways God spoke of old to our fathers by
  the prophets;
²but in these last days he has spoken to us by a Son,
    whom he appointed the heir of all things,
       through whom also he created the world.
       ³He reflects the glory of God and bears the very stamp
       of his nature,
       upholding the universe by his word of power.
    When he had made purification for sins,
    he sat down at the right of the Majesty on high,
⁴having become as much superior to angels
  as the name he has obtained is more excellent than theirs.

First we notice that the idea of God's speech is initially
presented in terms of the prophetic message, which signifies
God's revelation through preaching. This was previously given
through the prophets, but has now been given through God's
Son. In the light of 2.1–4 and 13.7 it is clear that Hebrews is
referring to the gospel message to which he wishes to recall his
readers. The gospel is thus continuous with the revelation of
God throughout history.

Next there is a deliberate contrast of the ages, which is an
indispensable presupposition of the argument which is to be
developed. The gospel belongs to the last days in distinction
from all the time that has preceded it. Here Hebrews reflects
the presuppositions of earliest Christianity, shared with Jewish
apocalyptic eschatology of the time, that God as creator and
controller of history has a predetermined plan. This reaches its
goal in the era of salvation, which is even now about to begin.
The plan has been revealed by God 'in many and various
ways', and the Old Testament Scriptures are the repository of
this revelation. The revelation concerned what God would do
at the end of the present age. The phrase 'in these last days' is
literally 'at the end of these days' and corresponds with a
Hebrew expression (*be-aharith hayyamim*) found in Gen. 49.1;
Isa. 2.2 and frequently in the prophets. In some of these
passages there is mention of the restoration of the monarchy,
i.e. the promise of the Messiah (e.g. Jer. 33.14–16), and this
had become a vivid expectation in New Testament times. But
it is more correct to think of it as God's intervention to save his

people, inaugurating a new era, in which the Messiah (if mentioned) is expected to take part. The rabbis speak of it as the Coming Age (*ha'olam habba'*) by contrast with the Present Age (*ha'olam hazzeh*). This eschatological understanding of history is constantly presupposed by Hebrews, however much he may use the language of a timeless contrast between earthly and heavenly or real and unreal. At this level of basic theology and cosmology Hebrews belongs to the mainstream of Jewish and Christian thought of his time.

Thirdly, it is absolutely vital for what is going to be argued in the body of the letter that this transition of the ages, marked by the coming of the Messiah and showing the fulfilment of prophecy, has actually arrived in the person of Jesus. In these verses the impression is given that his function as Messiah has been completed. This is indeed the case as far as 'purification of sins' is concerned. That will be indispensable for the subsequent argument. But Hebrews knows that the parousia and final judgment are still in the future (cf. 10.36–8), though he does not say so here. This again agrees with the primitive kerygma (cf. Paul's very simple statement of it in 1 Thess. 1.9–10).

Fourthly, though there is no doubt about the identification of the Messiah with Jesus, it is significant that Hebrews chooses to use the designation Son, and says 'a Son', not 'the Son'. As Westcott says, 'The absence of the article fixes attention upon the nature and not upon the personality of the mediator of the new revelation.'[5] By using this word Hebrews is able to combine two essential ideas. They are given in verse 2 in what may seem to be the wrong order, which will be put right in verse 3, thus creating the chiasmus. Thus 'whom he appointed the heir of all things' is eschatological, referring to the end time. From this point of view 'Son' is Messianic, as is clear from the quotation of Ps. 2.7 in verse 5, 'You are my Son, today I have begotten you.' This is in fact one of the Messianic proof-texts of the primitive church (cf. Acts 13.33). Hebrews here shows knowledge of the larger context of the quotation, for Ps. 2.8 continues, 'I will give you the nations for your inherit-

[5] B. F. Westcott, *The Epistle to the Hebrews* (London, 1889) *ad loc.*

ance.' But then, having made this eschatological reference, Hebrews introduces the other idea referring to the beginning of time: 'Through whom also he created the world'. Here we have a cosmic application of 'Son'. It is a personification of God's creative ability and activity as a helper, like Wisdom (usually personified as a woman) in such passages as Prov. 8.22–31 and Wisd. 7.22–8.1. Thus Hebrews correlates Son of God as Messiah with Son of God as his agent in the creation.

These two ideas are clarified in the right order in verses 3 and 4. We shall take first the cosmic idea, which raises important questions for the christology of Hebrews. Can it be regarded as part of the primitive kerygma? If not, at what point does it enter Christian thinking? What is the origin of the idea? And what does it mean for Hebrews? Does it imply the pre-existence of Jesus and a doctrine of incarnation comparable to the Prologue of John (John 1.1–18)?

It can be said at once that it is most unlikely that the cosmic idea of Jesus as the pre-existent Son of God figured in the earliest preaching, though it might well have formed part of the message of the original missionaries to the Hebrews church. The basis of it is the tendency to take an attribute to God, such as his creative wisdom, and to distinguish it from God conceptually as a mediating figure, his agent in creation. There is nothing un-Hebraic in this, for it is in line with such examples as the personification of the arm of the Lord in Isa. 51.9. But it comes to the fore in the post-exilic confrontation with Greek thought, because it provided a way of coping with the philosophical questions about the relationship between the world and God. It is in such a frontier situation that presentation of the gospel was likely to arouse cosmological questions, because the proclamation that Jesus has been raised to God's right hand as the Messiah already gives him a cosmic position. This question could have come to the surface in the Hellenistic Jewish circle around Stephen.

The beginnings of the idea can be seen in the work of Paul. Paul speaks of Jesus as 'Christ the power of God and the wisdom of God' (1 Cor. 1.24). Jesus is then the one in whom God's power and wisdom have been effectively displayed.

Then in Col. 1.15–17 there is a statement of it which is strikingly similar to our present passage in Hebrews.[6] If Colossians is not by Paul, it may be dated about the same time as Hebrews. In both passages the reference is to God's Son, and wisdom as such is not used. He is 'the first-born of all creation' (Col. 1.15, cf. Heb. 1.6). He is 'the image of the invisible God' (Col. 1.15, cf. Heb. 1.3a). 'All things were created through him and for him' (Col. 1.16; cf. Heb. 1.2c). The Colossians passage goes on to describe Jesus as 'the head of the body, the church ... the beginning, the first-born from the dead' (Col. 1.18), thus making a formal comparison between God's Son as the agent of creation and God's Son as the beginning of the new creation embodied in the church.

If we think of the creation as the product of God's power or Wisdom, or more precisely of his Word, seeing that God spoke (Gen. 1.3), we can see that it is possible to speak of this creative activity which brings the world to birth as God's 'first-born'. This goes happily with the personification of this attribute of God as his Son. This in its turn makes a simple link with the identification of Jesus as the Son of God in the sense of the Messiah, who is also referred to as God's first-born in Ps. 89.27. Thus Jesus can be represented as the one in whom God's Wisdom/Son/Word is definitively expressed. This almost amounts to the idea of incarnation, which has its one clear New Testament statement in the Prologue of John, with its assertion that the Word became flesh (John 1.14). Caird's judicious clarification of the christology of Hebrews, which follows these lines, warns us against imposing on Hebrews a theory of what incarnation means which he does not actually state.[7]

The groundwork for these similar statements in Colossians,

---

[6] Phil. 2.5–11 is another comparable christological statement, possibly a pre-Pauline composition, and likely to be earlier than Colossians. But it is not clear how far the opening verses are intended to imply pre-existence or are indebted to the Wisdom tradition: cf. J. D. G. Dunn, *Christology in the Making* (London, 1980), pp. 114–21.

[7] G. B. Caird, 'Son by Appointment', in W. C. Weinrich (ed.), *The New Testament Age: Essays in Honor of Bo Reicke* (2 vols., Macon, GA, 1984), I, pp. 73–81; cf. L. D. Hurst, 'The Christology of Hebrews 1 and 2', in L. D. Hurst and N. T. Wright (ed.), *The Glory of Christ in the New Testament; Studies in Christology in Memory of G. B. Caird* (Oxford, 1987), pp. 151–64.

Hebrews, and John, which are independent of each other from a literary point of view, had been laid by Alexandrian Judaism. Hebrews is probably directly indebted to Wisd. 7.26: 'For she is a reflection of eternal light, a spotless mirror of the working of God, and an image of his goodness.' It is less likely that Hebrews made any direct use of Philo, but there are many similar phrases. Thus Philo (*Plant.* 1. 332) holds that the rational (*logikē*) soul is comparable to the seal of God, 'whose stamp is the eternal word (*logos*)'. Philo personifies the *logos* as a son of God as part of a widely ranging and fluctuating use of metaphors which helps us to see how these ideas were available to Christian thinkers among the Hellenistic converts.[8]

So does Hebrews think of the pre-existence of *Jesus?* The above considerations suggest that he did not quite do so, or did so only in a limited sense. He thinks of the pre-existent Son of God, active in the creation and expressed partially in the prophets, and expressed fully and finally in the man Jesus. This is probably the clue to the disputed words in Heb. 1.6, 'when he brings the first-born into the world'. In this action of God the angels are bidden to 'worship him'. But what occasion is referred to? Jewish tradition in *The Life of Adam and Eve* 13–15 declares that when Adam and Eve were created in the image and likeness of God, God commanded the angels to worship them.[9] This might suggest that the incarnation is meant in the case of Jesus. But the stress should not be placed on the moment of birth, but on the significance of who he is. When the pre-existent Wisdom/Son/Word reaches the fullest expression in the Jesus of history, the angels are to worship, for here they see the reflection of God himself, the one in whom and through whom god's predetermined plan of salvation is accomplished, and who has therefore rightly 'sat down at the right hand of the Majesty on high'. Thus the 'first-born' is introduced to the world of humanity in the

[8] For Logos in Philo see Williamson, *Philo*, pp. 386–495.
[9] The text in English translation is given in J. H. Charlesworth, *The Old Testament Pseudepigrapha* (2 vols., London, 1983–5), II, pp. 258–95. The passage referred to is on p. 262. The book is believed to date from the late first century AD.

whole process of the saving events of which Jesus is God's
agent.

Jesus the Messiah

It has already been pointed out that the unifying factor in the
presentation of Jesus in these opening verses is the designation
'Son of God'. This brings together the Wisdom christology,
which we have just considered, and the Messiahship of Jesus.
For 'Son of God' is a designation of the Messiah based on Ps.
2.7 (quoted in Heb. 1.5) and other Messianic passages, and
'first-born' in 1.6 may well be a literary allusion to Ps. 89.27:
'And I will make him the first-born, the highest of the kings of
the earth.' These words immediately follow a verse which
closely resembles 2 Sam. 7.14, just quoted in 1.5b. Then in
1.8–9 a further Messianic text is adduced (Ps. 45.6–7) so as to
emphasise the enthronement of Jesus as heavenly Lord. As
already noted, Hebrews here reproduces the apostolic proclamation that Jesus is the Messiah and builds on a well-
established tradition of proof-texts in support of it.[10]

The point which we must now observe is that the Messianic
use of 'Son of God' relates not so much to divine origin as to
divine status. The question of origin (not raised in the earliest
preaching) was solved with the aid of the Wisdom tradition, as
we have just seen. The question of status was raised during the
ministry of Jesus (cf. Mark 8.27–9;14.61), and it is still not
clear how far he claimed to be the expected Messiah.[11] But
there can be no doubt that this claim was made in the apostolic
kerygma on the basis of the resurrection. This remains true,
however much the precise form of that event eludes historical
investigation.[12] Theologically the resurrection is only the
centre-piece of three linked events, crucifixion, resurrection,

---

[10] Cf. B. Lindars, *New Testament Aplologetic* (London, 1961).

[11] Recent books on Jesus which take this problem into account include J. Riches, *Jesus and the Transformation of Judaism* (London, 1980), J. Ziesler, *The Jesus Question* (Guildford and London, 1980), A. E. Harvey, *Jesus and the Constraints of History* (London, 1982), and E. P. Sanders, *Jesus and Judaism* (London, 1985).

[12] The problems of the NT resurrection traditions are set out trenchantly by T. Sheehan, *The First Coming* (New York, 1986), pp. 89–73.

and exaltation. In the apostolic preaching Jesus is not regarded
as Messiah apart from all three of these events. This explains
why it was so important to prove from Scripture that, contrary
to common expectation, the Messiah must die before achieving
his Messianic work. The chief source used was the prophecy of
the Suffering Servant in Isaiah 53. Hebrews alludes to it in
9.28.[13] The use of this prophecy also reinforced the positive
understanding of the death of Jesus as an atoning sacrifice.
Then the resurrection and ascension of Jesus anticipate in his
person the general resurrection (cf. 1 Cor. 15.23), and his
heavenly session at the right hand of God places him in
readiness to act on behalf of God in the eschatological events,
which are his proper Messianic functions. This also was
proved from Scripture. The key text is Ps. 110.1, which is
widely quoted or alluded to in the New Testament, and from
which the formula of sitting at the right hand of God is derived.
Hebrews alludes to it in 1.3 and quotes it in 1.13.[14]

From the point of view of status the emphasis naturally falls
on the heavenly session, because that completes the process
which establishes the Messiahship of Jesus. This is a matter of
the greatest importance for Hebrews. In our glimpse of the
overall argument we have seen that the crucial question is
whether the sacrificial death of Jesus has lasting efficacy so as
to deal with sins now. Hence the central argument will expound
the heavenly session from this point of view (cf. 10.11–14,
alluding again to Ps. 110.1). This also explains the emphasis
on the permanence of the heavenly session expressed in the
quotations of Ps. 45.6–7 and 102.25–7 in 1.8–12.[15] On the other

---

[13] The allusion is to Isa. 53.12; cf. 1 Pet. 2.24. The idea of the intercession of Jesus in
7.25 probably alludes to the same verse in the original Hebrew (the LXX differs). If
so, Hebrews derived it from traditional usage; cf. Rom. 8.34.

[14] Cf. D. M. Hay, *Glory at the Right Hand: Psalm 110 in Early Christianity* (New York and
Nashville, 1973). There are many allusions to this psalm in Hebrews in addition to
these two direct quotations.

[15] Ps. 45.6–7 appears to be addressed to God, but the context suggests the king, whom
Hebrews identifies with the Messiah. Ps. 102.25–7 is certainly addressed to God. In
applying it to Jesus, Hebrews follows an established procedure in which texts
referring to God as 'Lord' (the regular substitute for the divine name in reading the
OT) are applied to Jesus as his agent: cf. Wilson, pp. 42f. There is another example
in 1.6, where Deut. 32.43 (LXX) refers to the worship of God in the original
context; see also the use of Isa. 45.23 in Phil. 2.10–11.

hand there is only the slightest reference to the sacrificial death in the opening verses ('When he had made purification for sins', 1.3c), though it is part of the common faith accepted by the readers. But it is also the focus of the dispute. At this early stage in his address Hebrews does not want to alienate his readers by introducing the subject too prominently.

There is also a glaring gap in 1.3, inasmuch as the resurrection is omitted altogether. Moreover, it is never mentioned in the body of the letter. However, it is referred to in the formula of blessing at the end (13.20). If this is an integral part of the letter and not a later interpolation (which is not really very likely),[16] the explanation must be that it did not seem necessary to mention it separately, seeing that it is implied by the juxtaposition of death and exaltation. Thus, whereas the death is alluded to just briefly, giving a hint of the theme which will be treated so fully later on, the resurrection is simply assumed, because it will not receive special treatment in the subsequent argument.

Jesus and the angels

The Messianic status of Jesus is highlighted by being set in contrast with the angels (1.4). Then the contrast becomes a major theme in 1.5–14, in which all the Messianic passages serve the purpose of proving the subordinate status of the angels. This at first sight seems entirely unnecessary, especially as the theme will not be taken up again in the rest of the letter, apart from what immediately follows in 2.1–10. It was suggested by T. W. Manson that the aim is to combat a tendency among the readers to worship angels, thus reflecting a possible interpretation of the complaint against the Colossians in Col. 2.18.[17] But there is no hint of this elsewhere in Hebrews, and the idea goes against the observation that at this

---

[16] Doubts have been expressed about the integrity of 13.20–1 because of its different tone from the rest (see Spicq, II, p. 434), but that is due to the literary form. In fact nearly every phrase picks up an idea used earlier in the letter, and only the resurrection and the shepherd metaphor are without parallel.

[17] T.W. Manson, 'The Problem of the Epistle to the Hebrews', *Studies in the Gospels and Epistles* (Manchester, 1962), pp. 242ff.

early stage in the letter Hebrews is recalling agreed positions. Another suggestion is that he is opposing an angel christology, attributed to the Jewish–Christian sect of the Ebionites by Epiphanius.[18] This makes Jesus himself an angel, in fact the lord of the angels. It probably arose in a Jewish setting with an advanced doctrine of angels, such as we can see in the Dead Sea Scrolls and apocalyptic literature, and was developed in order to avoid any infringement of the monotheistic under-standing of God.[19] But again it is a mistake to see a deliberate polemic against false views here.

The real reason for the contrast becomes plain in 2.1–10. It is here that Hebrews first suggests that his readers may have strayed from the original teaching. In doing so he compares another range of teaching, 'the message declared by angels' (2.2). This means the Jewish Law, which was held in con-temporary Jewish teaching to have been delivered to Moses by the mediation of an angel (Acts 7.38, 53; Gal. 3.19).[20] This takes us to the heart of the problem, because the readers were tempted to resort to the Law to cope with their consciousness of sin. One way of expressing the superiority of the Christian teaching is to show the superiority of Jesus over the angels. It also suggests the finality of the new teaching and its absolute effectiveness in relation to God's plan of salvation. The angels are merely ministering spirits (1.14), unlike the Son of God, who is eternal (1.8–13), and the Law similarly has only a subordinate role in the history of salvation.

The humanity of Jesus

After using this contrast of Law and gospel so as to give a first hint of the problem that is to be tackled in the letter, Hebrews brilliantly introduces another contrast involving the angels, the contrast between their position and the destiny of the

---

[18] Epiphanius, *Pan.* 30.16.4. Cf. J. D. G. Dunn, *Unity and Diversity in the New Testament* (London, 1977), p. 242; Wilson, pp. 33f.

[19] Thus in 11QMelchizedek Melchizedek (= the angel Michael in this document) performs the eschatological judgment on behalf of God.

[20] In Jewish sources the idea appears in *Jub.* 2.17–9; CD 5.18; Josephus, *Ant.* xv.136; *Sifre* Num 102; *Mekhilta* Ex 20.18; *Pesikta rabbati* 21.

human race. There is no warrant in Scripture for supposing that the angels will have the status of the Messiah as heavenly lord, as indicated in Ps. 110.1, just quoted in 1.13. On the other hand a related text, already associated with it in the early Christian use of Scripture, makes this contrast explicit. This is Ps. 8.4–6 in the Septuagint version, which Hebrews quotes in 2.6–8. Its use elsewhere is attested in similar contexts in 1 Cor. 15.27 and Eph. 1.22. Here the point is that the human race is lower in the order of creation than the angels, but destined to be 'crowned with glory and honour'. This is one of the places where the argument appears to turn on the Greek form of the text, because the Septuagint 'angels' translates *elohim*, which normally means 'God' or 'the gods'. On the other hand it may be the actual meaning of the passage, and in any case accords with the contemporary Jewish exegesis.[21]

Hebrews first shows how this has been fulfilled in Jesus himself. Made, like all human beings, 'lower than the angels', he has passed through death to the position of glory and honour. But this is in order to be the means of bringing all the rest of humanity to the same position. Hebrews fully understands that 'man' and 'son of man' in the psalm are collective terms, even though he interprets them individually of Jesus in the first instance.[22] Here we should note in passing that there is no indication at all that he regards 'son of man' as a Messianic title. The problem of Son of Man in the sayings of Jesus in the Gospels is too large a topic to be treated here. It must suffice to say that the use of the phrase as a title for the exalted Messiah (as, for instance, in Mark 14.62) would not be incompatible with the thought of Hebrews, but he certainly does not do so, and he does not seem to be aware even

[21] The interpretation 'angels' may well be correct, because the plural form *elohim* = 'God' (plural of majesty) or 'gods' can be used more generally for divine beings: cf. 1 Sam. 28.13 (the spirit of Samuel); Ps. 82.1, 6 (understood as the angels in 11QMelchizedek). However, in Ps. 8.5 the later versions of the Greek OT (Aquila, Symmachus, and Theodotion) have 'God'.

[22] The words used are *anthropos (enosh)* and *huios anthropou (ben adam)*, but Hebrews does not bring into the discussion the first man, Adam. Thus I am not convinced that this is an example of the Adam christology developed by Paul, as argued by Dunn (*Christology*, pp. 98–128).

of the possibility of doing so. He values the phrase solely as a means of pointing out the solidarity of Jesus with the human race.[23]

The real humanity of Jesus is essential for the argument of Hebrews, because the whole argument turns on the saving efficacy of his death. It is, of course, yet another point which he can take as common ground. The original teaching never denied that Jesus was human, and there is no reason to suppose that the readers would have done so, unlike some of the later Gnostic heretics. Thus it is not possible for Hebrews to remain faithful to the tradition and at the same time to develop an argument which leaves the humanity of Jesus out of account. In fact he uses it to great advantage. For the solidarity of Jesus with humanity makes him a representative figure. He is the 'pioneer' (2.10) of the way of salvation for the whole human race.[24] As such he has completed the process through his death, resurrection, and exaltation. We shall see later that the idea of perfection, which is a favourite expression of Hebrews, really refers to the *completion of the process of salvation*. This has been accomplished first in Jesus, and through him will be accomplished in all believers. So he is not only the pioneer but also the representative of all humanity. From this point of view he can be referred to metaphorically as a high priest (2.17).

It is important to realise that this first mention of the highpriesthood of Jesus is only a metaphor at this stage. It will become a serious proposition in the subsequent argument. Because it is mentioned here almost casually, as if it is already known to the readers, Rissi assumes that Hebrews was not the

---

[23] Though Bruce wishes to see here an allusion to the Son of Man title, more recent work on the problem suggests that there was no such title in the christology of early Christianity, but that it is a development within the sayings tradition of the Gospels. The phrase properly means simply 'a human being'. See G. Vermes, *Jesus the Jew* (London, 1973), pp. 160–91; M. Casey, *Son of Man* (London, 1979); B. Lindars, *Jesus Son of Man* (London, 1983).

[24] The Greek *archēgos* is used of Jesus twice in Acts (3.15; 5.31). In the latter passage it operates virtually as a Messianic title, and invites comparison with the use of Hebrew *nasi'* in the Scrolls. However, it is common in Greek literature to denote an originator or founder (Plato, Josephus), and should be regarded as a non-technical word which Hebrews uses to express his meaning.

first to use it, so that the origin of it must be sought elsewhere.[25] But this view fails to take into account the rhetoric of Hebrews. The aim is to introduce the idea gently and in an acceptable manner. If the readers consider the implications of the humanity of Jesus, which they accept in any case, they will realise that there is a sense in which he can be described as a high priest. This in its turn enables Hebrews to reintroduce the idea of the purification of sins, which he had just mentioned in 1.3, for it is the proper function of a high priest 'to make expiation for the sins of the people' (2.17). This is the crucial issue, which is tempting the readers to hark back to Judaism to deal with their sins. So it is not without a side-glance at the readers themselves that Hebrews points out that the humanity of Jesus covers temptation too: 'For because he himself has suffered and been tempted, he is able to help those who are tempted' (2.18).

Conclusion

The basic theology of Hebrews stands in line with the apostolic kerygma so far as it can be deduced from the New Testament writings. Jesus is remembered as a man of recent history, who died for our sins and rose and was glorified. Sitting at the right hand of God, he is reserved in heaven to be the agent of God in the general resurrection and the judgment, still felt to be imminent (10.25, 37). All this accords with the predetermined plan of God, which has been made known in advance through the Scriptures.

Hebrews goes beyond the most primitive proclamation in seeing Jesus as the one in whom the Wisdom/Son/Word of God has its ultimate expression, but this view is shared with other Christians in a Hellenistic milieu (Paul, Colossians, and John). This form of christology is often referred to by modern scholars as adoptionism so as to distinguish it from incarnation, which is truly reached only in John. But the distinction is a narrow one and ought not to be pressed. Because Wisdom/Son/Word is the personification of an attribute of God which refers to his activity, we are here dealing with a dynamic idea,

[25] Rissi, *Theologie*, p. 55. See also ch. 1, n. 1 above.

and it makes very little difference whether we think of it as
expressed in Jesus or embodied (enfleshed) in him. Moreover it
is inevitable that the personification of this attribute as the Son
of God should be pictured in terms of Jesus, who used to call
God his Father and is now exalted as the Messianic Son of
God. In this way Jesus himself can be spoken of as pre-existent,
and this leads to the classic idea of Jesus as the Son of God who
leaves his throne in heaven to become man and resumes it after
his death and resurrection. It is not clear, however, that this
idea has been reached in Hebrews.[26]

In Hebrews we can see christology developing along this
line, to become the groundwork for later dogmatic formula-
tions. But it has little bearing on the aspects of theology which
are central to the purpose of Hebrews. These are the sacrificial
death of Jesus and its soteriological and eschatological significance.

THE WAY TO PERFECTION

In the first two chapters of his letter Hebrews has set out his
basic understanding of the person and work of Christ. This
forms the foundation for his exposition of the continuing
effectiveness of the atoning death of Jesus, which is the
essential point for his readers to grasp. Before coming to this,
however, he explains in chapters 3 and 4 the aim of the
Christian life. This is participation in the completion of God's
plan of salvation, referred to metaphorically in 4.9 as the
'sabbath rest for the people of God'. These two chapters thus
give further preliminary considerations which are required for
the following argument. From the point of view of the rhetorical structure of the letter they serve two purposes. On the
one hand they give the larger context of the meaning of
Christian discipleship within which the particular problem of
the readers has arisen. On the other hand they provide the
means of sharpening the rebuke to the readers, which has been
suggested only very gently so far. This is put strongly in
4.11–13, and the implication is that the readers are liable to

[26] Cf. Dunn, *Christology*, p. 237.

'fall by the same sort of disobedience' as the Israelites in the wilderness. But this only makes the christological point, that the human Christ 'is able to help those who are tempted' (2.18), more relevant. Thus it is repeated more strongly immediately after the rebuke in 4.14–16. And the fact that Jesus 'has been tempted as we are, yet without sinning' (4.15) relates directly to the central issue, that the readers are tempted to 'fall by the same sort of disobedience' because of their inability to come to terms with their consciousness of sin.

Hebrews is dealing with a delicate pastoral issue. The readers are not wilfully and defiantly disobedient, but deeply troubled in conscience and strongly moved to resort to the help of the Jewish community. One aspect of the problem is their failure to understand the full implications of the faith which they profess. So these two chapters give a broad view of the Christian life, laying particular emphasis on the quality of faith, i.e. faithfulness to the confession (3.2, 6, 14; 4.14). The importance of this for the main argument will become clear when Hebrews reintroduces the theme of faith at the climax of the argument in chapters 10–12. The virtue of faith is not merely a matter of loyalty to a position once taken up, but the essential response from the heart which actually solves the whole problem, as we shall then see.

For the purpose of our present study it will be useful to look at some of the presuppositions of what Hebrews is saying here, as they provide further aspects of his underlying theology which are needed for the following argument. These will be grouped under the headings of the idea of perfection, the old and the new, the use of Scripture in Hebrews, and the Holy Spirit.

The idea of perfection

This idea, which has been the subject of a very useful study by D. Peterson,[27] is more prominent in Hebrews than may appear at first sight because it is expressed with the aid of several different Greek words formed from the same root and requires

[27] D. Peterson, *Hebrews and Perfection* (Cambridge, 1982).

a variety of English words in translation. These words are derived from *telos* = end (conclusion) or goal (outcome), which is used only four times in Hebrews, always with the meaning 'end' (3.14; 6.8, 11; 7.3).[28] But the verb *teleioō* = make perfect, and other words from the same stem (*teleios, teleiotēs, teleiōsis, teleiōtēs*), are common, and are important for the theology of Hebrews.

It has already been pointed out above that perfection in Hebrews means the completion of God's plan of salvation. This brings all the examples under one heading, and suits the intention of the argument as a whole. Though Hebrews is deeply concerned about the conquest of sin, he does not use the idea of perfection to denote the moral ideal, except in so far as that is entailed in the completion of God's plan. Accepting the determinism of apocalyptic eschatology and the cosmic implications of the Wisdom christology, he sees the whole historical process teleologically, moving towards completion, fullness, and perfection. This is not a doctrine of progress in the humanist sense, suggesting inevitable advance towards the realisation of the superman. It is in fact a two-stage process. The first is the era of the old covenant, which is due to pass away (8.14). The second is the coming age or end time, in which the new covenant will come into operation. The message of the gospel is that the new age has been inaugurated in the person of Christ. Thus the transition from the old age to the new has already taken place in Jesus, and the object of the Christian life is to enable all people to enter the new age too.

With this general idea in mind, Hebrews can speak of the perfecting of Jesus himself. Through his death the process has been completed in Jesus himself, thus blazing the trail for all the rest of humanity: 'For it was fitting that he, for whom and by whom all things exist, in bringing many sons to glory, should make the pioneer of their salvation perfect (*teleiōsai*) through suffering' (2.10). It has been suggested that the verb here has a technical sense used in the Greek mystery religions,

---

[28] Many manuscripts add 'firm to the end (*telos*)' to the end of 3.6, but this is probably due to the influence of 3.14. It is not found in the most ancient texts.

i.e. to initiate or consecrate a person in the mysteries.[29] But this suggestion rests on a misunderstanding of what Hebrews is saying. The context shows that the death of Jesus is the means whereby he reaches the position of glory which belongs to the completion of the process (2.9), and the point is that his death is also the means of bringing all people to the same position. This is then expressed with the *metaphor* of sanctifying in the next verse (2.11), using the normal biblical word *hagiazō*. It prepares the ground for the metaphor of priesthood in 2.17. Thus the idea of perfection here is applied to the glory of Jesus which results from his death. It is the position which belongs to the completion of God's plan. There is, of course, no use of the moral sense of perfection here, because there is no suggestion that Jesus was previously imperfect morally, though he was tempted like everyone else (4.15).

Jesus is the 'pioneer' of our salvation, because he has completed the process first. He is also the 'perfecter (*teleiōtēs*) of our faith' (12.2), because he enables those who hold fast to the Christian profession to reach the same goal. This has two sides to it, because it is necessary to show both how the death of Jesus is effective in itself for the purpose and also how the people on their part may appropriate what has been done on their behalf. The readers have apparently lost confidence in the first point, at least as regards atonement for post-baptismal sin. So Hebrews points out that perfection (*teleiōsis*) cannot be attained through the sacrifices of the Levitical priesthood (7.11). Indeed 'the law made nothing perfect' (7.19). On the other hand the sacrifice of Jesus is permanently effective: 'For by a single offering he has perfected for all time those who are sanctified' (10.14), whereas the sacrifices under the Law 'can never ... make perfect those who draw near' (10.1).

Similarly the readers have a defective understanding of the method of appropriating what Jesus has done for them. This will be shown to be faith, expounded in chapters 10–12. Thus from both points of view what is needed is maturity of

---

[29] The possibility was observed by Westcott (p. 65) and taken up with enthusiasm by Käsemann, *Das wandernde Gottesvolk*, for his Gnostic theory of Hebrews, but is generally rejected by modern critics.

understanding. So, before embarking on the main argument on these matters, which begins with chapter 7, Hebrews urges them to be 'mature' as opposed to being like children (5.14) and to 'go on to maturity' (6.1). But the words he uses for 'mature' and 'maturity' are literally 'perfect' (*teleios*) and 'perfection' (*teleiotēs*). What they need is *complete understanding*, suitable to the aim of reaching completion of the process of salvation. Thus the way of perfection is not a self-conscious individualist spirituality of overcoming little sins, but the completion of God's plan for everyone. In fact Hebrews does not think of the readers individually, but is always concerned with what applies to them all as members of the group.[30]

This helps us to see a fundamental difference between Hebrews and Philo. Though some of his ideas have parallels in the writings of Philo, the aim is entirely different. Hebrews is not in the least concerned with Philo's central preoccupation with the life of virtue and religious experience. Hebrews is concerned with the act of God himself which has opened up the 'new and living way' (10.20) to the heavenly sanctuary.[31] This means the presence of God. So we shall see that, out of all the ideas that are used to express the notion of the coming age, the leading thought for Hebrews is *direct access to God*, and this means having heart and mind open to God with no barrier to break the relationship. It is well known that Jewish apocalyptic is reticent about the life of the coming age, and what is given in the literary descriptions is intended to be understood symbolically. This is obvious in Revelation 21. Elsewhere in the New Testament the apocalyptic passages stop short of describing what follows the general resurrection and the judgment (see Mark 13 and 1 Corinthians 15, etc.). Hebrews talks about 'glory' and 'salvation', which are conventional words. But when he wishes to give positive content to the idea of the future existence, it is the language of direct access to God that he uses

[30] This point is made emphatically by Käsemann, *Das wandernde Gottesvolk*, p. 8.
[31] The eschatology of Hebrews is fundamental, and constitutes the decisive difference between Hebrews and Philo. This is most interestingly set out (with reference also to the *Epistle of Barnabas*) by C. K. Barrett, 'The Eschatology of the Epistle to the Hebrews', in W. D. Davies and D. Daube (eds.), *The Background of the New Testament and its Eschatology: Studies in Honour of C. H. Dodd* (Cambridge, 1956), pp. 363–93.

(for instance 6.19–20). This is important for a proper understanding of the central argument on atonement in chapters
7–10. But it is also important as another link with the primitive
kerygma, because it ties up with the religious teaching of Jesus
himself in his proclamation of the presence of God.[32] So the
goal of direct access to God has been completed in Jesus
through his sacrificial death, and this event has opened the
way towards the same goal for those who approach God
through him (8.25).[33]

The old and the new

Because the completion of God's plan is a matter of the
transition from the present age (which is continuous with the
past) to the Coming Age, the contrast of old and new is
frequently deployed in the argument. I have just referred to the
old covenant and the new covenant, and this will receive more
attention later. But it has broader aspects, and some of these
need to be considered as a preliminary to our study of the use of
Scripture in Hebrews. For his main argument on the atoning
death of Jesus, Hebrews will have to make constant use of
Scripture at the same time as arguing for a position which
regards it as superseded. He prepares the ground for this in
chapters 3 and 4 by setting before the readers the main aim of
the spiritual life in terms of an example from the Old
Testament.

In these chapters Moses is held up as an example of the
fidelity which can be seen in Jesus and ought to be characteristic of the readers. God's promise of the land of Canaan is
contrasted with the promise of salvation which is set before

---

[32] See recent books on Jesus (n. 11 above). A crucial text is Mark 9.1, in which the
coming of the kingdom of God in strength is a surrogate expression for the coming of
God himself, as demonstrated by B. D. Chilton, *God in Strength* (reprint, Sheffield,
1987).

[33] Hebrews expresses the concept of direct access to God in terms of entry into the
heavenly sanctuary, but of course this is metaphorical language. Some (e.g. Rissi)
have argued that Hebrews is opposing the desire of the readers to achieve access
through mystical experience. But if the central issue is removing the barrier of sin, it
is better to think of it as an ethical relationship, maintained now by faith and made
permanent in the completion of God's plan at the parousia.

them in the gospel. The disobedience of the Israelites in the journey through the wilderness is used as an object lesson for the readers in their particular situation.

Everything that is said here is likely to accord sufficiently well with the presuppositions of the readers to win their assent, and so to predispose them to accept the argument which is to follow. At the same time each item is a necessary preliminary to the argument itself.

First the example of faith. This means fidelity to the confession that Jesus is the Christ (13.7–8). This is a characteristic of Jesus himself, so that he is entitled to be called 'the apostle and high priest of our confession' (3.1). The word 'apostle', used of Jesus only here in the New Testament, has its proper meaning of delegate or accredited representative (see Matt. 10.40; John 13.20), and prepares for the comparison with Moses.[34] By adding 'and high priest of our confession' Hebrews maintains the essential concept of priesthood, which must not be allowed to drop out of the argument. He will return to it in 4.14–16, which makes an artistic inclusion with 3.1. The two concepts of apostle and high priest denote the vocation of Jesus to which he was faithful, thus qualifying him to be the object of the confession of faith. This is the indispensable quality for the readers themselves. In commending it to his readers (3.6), Hebrews adduces the example of Moses from Num. 12.7, where Moses is singled out for his faithfulness. This is calculated to appeal to the readers, who obviously retain great respect for him as the giver of the Law. But the same passage also provides the opportunity to point up the contrast between Moses and Jesus. Moses is described as God's servant, whereas Jesus is God's Son (3.6). Thus Jesus is a better example to follow and his role ranks higher than that of Moses. This type of comparison and contrast will be used constantly in the main argument.

Secondly Numbers 12 is a story of disobedience on the part of others, and so paves the way for the example of the disobedience of the Israelites which jeopardised the goal of reaching the promised land. This must be regarded as a

[34] See the classic treatment of *apostolos* by K. H. Rengstorf, *TDNT*, I, pp. 407–47.

standing example in Jewish moral teaching, also echoed in
1 Cor. 10.1–13 by Paul. According to Num. 14.21–3 the whole
generation of those who began the journey were wiped out
before the land was reached except Joshua and Caleb.
Hebrews makes this point by citing Ps. 95.7–11, which refers
to God's severe decision to do this. But the psalm takes the
form of addressing later generations, exhorting them not to
behave in the same way. This makes the application to the
readers simple and effective. They too must not 'harden their
hearts'. Otherwise they are liable to forfeit the goal. In the
psalm this is described not as the promised land but as God's
rest (*katapausis*). Applied to the readers it gives a new image
for the completion of God's plan, the state of direct access to
God.

It is easy to see that Hebrews has found an excellent moral
example for his purpose, which is likely to be familiar to his
readers, and to which they can respond. But it also has theological significance. The jump from the historical setting in
the wilderness to their present situation is not merely a matter
of moral example or allegorical equivalence. It depends on
taking the actual text seriously. For of course Hebrews takes
Psalm 95 as the utterance of King David, and David lived
long after the conquest of the promised land (4.7). Therefore
it is addressed to later generations, and when it refers to God's
'rest' as future, this must mean the eschatological future
(4.8–9). Moreover God is the speaker in the psalm, and he
refers to exclusion from '*my* rest' (4.3). Taking this literally as
God's own rest, Hebrews equates it with the fact that 'God ...
rested (LXX *katepausen*) on the seventh day' of creation (Gen.
2.2). This gives the clue to the nature of the new age: 'There
remains a sabbath rest (*sabbatismos*) for the people of God'
(4.9). This is a metaphor for something which cannot be
described literally. But it is meant seriously in that in Psalm
95 God has revealed his intention for the future, and according to the gospel message this has become available through
Christ.

The word *sabbatismos* does not occur in Greek literature
before Plutarch, and Spicq has suggested that Hebrews coined

it himself.[35] But the idea that the sabbath is 'the image of
the world to come' (*Genesis Rabba* 17 (12a)) is known from
rabbinic sources, and can be traced back into New Testament
times in the use of *katapausis* to denote the eschatological future
in the romance of *Joseph and Asenath* (8.9; 15.7; 22.13).[36] It was
thus available to provide one more designation of the coming
'perfection', the coming direct access to God in the Messianic
era of the new covenant. But its use here is derived from the
argument based on Psalm 95, and Hebrews does not take it up
again.

The point that is stressed, however, is that the new era
differs altogether from the previous era, and the readers are
warned that they could miss it at the judgment if they fail to
learn the lesson of those who were disobedient or unfaithful.
The warning in 4.11–13 is sharper and more terrifying than the
previous exhortations – but only to be followed by the assurance that the way of divine mercy remains open precisely
because of the highpriestly act of Jesus (4.14–16).

The use of Scripture in Hebrews

We have now seen several examples of the use of Scripture in
Hebrews, and so this seems to be a suitable point to give more
attention to this aspect of his theology.[37] It is commonly
asserted that Hebrews makes use of allegorical interpretation
of the Old Testament. At first sight this appears to be the

---

[35] Greek-speaking Jews transliterated the Hebrew *shabbath* as *sabbaton*, and the verb
sabbatizō = 'to keep sabbath' occurs several times in the LXX. In Plutarch, *Moralia*
166a, *sabbatismos* means 'sabbath-keeping', mentioned in a list of superstitious
practices. This suggests that the word was already current, and makes it less likely
that Hebrews coined it.

[36] The references are to the edition of C. Burchard and his English translation in
Charlesworth, *Pseudepigrapha*, II, pp. 202–47. In 8.9 Joseph's prayer for Asenath
includes the petition 'Let her enter your rest (*katapausis*) which you have prepared
for your chosen ones.' *Joseph and Asenath* is now held to have been composed in Egypt
between 100 BC and AD 100.

[37] There is a full study of the use of Scripture in Hebrews in F. Schröger, *Der Verfasser
des Hebräerbriefes als Schriftausleger* (Regensburg, 1968). We shall not be concerned
here with the relationship of Hebrews' quotations to the textual tradition of the
LXX (see K. J. Thomas, 'The Old Testament Citations in Hebrews', *NTS*, 11
(1965), 303–25; J. C. McCullough, 'The Old Testament Quotations in Hebrews',
NTS, 26 (1980), 332–46).

obvious explanation of the detailed application of the sacrificial laws of Leviticus to the death of Christ, which is so prominent in the crucial argument of chapters 7–10. However, it is certainly not allegory in the sense which applies to Philo, who treats the narratives and laws of the Pentateuch symbolically, applying them to the virtues and vices of the soul, which he considers to be their true spiritual meaning. Moreover, the example which we have just seen in the treatment of Psalm 95 shows that the basis of interpretation is eschatological. The Old Testament has meaning for the new era in so far as it reveals God's will for the future. We should thus be wary of accepting the common assumption that Hebrews uses a Platonic model, in which present earthly phenomena are shadows of eternal realities, in spite of such an apparently explicit statement as 10.1: 'For since the law has but a shadow of the good things to come instead of the true form of these realities, it can never ... make perfect those who draw near.' The language may be Platonic, but the idea is strictly temporal in accordance with Jewish and Christian eschatology. This is clear in the idea of 'the good things to come', but also applies to the idea of perfection, as we have seen.

This distinction may be grasped more easily if we observe that for the Platonic model earthly phenomena are the forms which correspond with the eternal ideas, whereas for Hebrews they are partial and temporary manifestations of God's *intentions*. From this point of view they may give valuable guidance with regard to the future. This is so, in Hebrews' understanding, in the case of the Levitical ceremonial for the Day of Atonement. He treats it seriously as God's preparatory revelation. It gives the proper basis for understanding the nature of sacrifice, which can be used to expose the sacrificial character of the death of Jesus. More broadly it can be asserted that the Old Testament supplies all the necessary definitions to which Jesus must conform to qualify for his role as high priest and sacrificial victim. It is important to observe that this in no way denies the value of the literal sense of the Old Testament.[38] It was valid for its own time, but that was the preparatory

[38] Cf. Spicq, I, p. 341.

dispensation. When the same principles are applied in relation to the new situation it is necessary to make various adjustments appropriate to the new conditions.

Another point which has already appeared in our study of Hebrews is his affiliation to the primitive church's use of Scripture in the apostolic kerygma. Messianic and eschatological prophecies obviously refer to the future and are fulfilled in Jesus, or are in process of fulfilment as a result of his saving work. In considering the christology of Hebrews we saw his use of some of the classic passages in chapter 1, notably Ps. 2.7 and 110.1. One aspect of his creative genius is to be seen in his further development of such traditional texts. His use of Ps. 110.4 ('You are a priest for ever after the order of Melchizedek') is both central to his argument and unique in the New Testament. On the other hand it is probable, in view of 1 Cor. 15.25–7, that Ps. 8.6 had already been adduced as a comment on Ps. 110.1. Hebrews uses this in 2.6–8 in relation to the destiny of humanity, which is fulfilled already in the person of Jesus.

The use of one text to illuminate another is of course common rabbinic practice, and we have just seen another example of it in relation to God's 'rest' in chapter 4. Other techniques which reflect rabbinic exegesis are the catena, or chain, of texts in chapter 1 (*haraz*) and the *a fortiori* argument in 9.13–14 (*qal wa-homer*). It has even been suggested that Hebrews was guided in his choice of texts by the Jewish lectionary in the synagogue, but this cannot be more than conjecture.[39]

The identification of Jesus with the Messiah not only encouraged the earliest Christians to discover how the Messianic prophecies were fulfilled in him, but also enlarged the scope of what was considered to be prophetic. Reinterpretation of Scripture begins within the Old Testament itself (for instance Dan. 9.2, 24–7 on Jer. 25.12). Eschatological interpre-

---

[39] The suggestion was made by A. Guilding, *The Fourth Gospel and Jewish Worship* (Oxford, 1960), p. 72, and also by C. H. Cave, 'The Influences of the Lectionary of the Synagogue on the Formation of the Epistle to the Hebrews' (unpublished M. A. dissertation, Nottingham, 1960).

tation of whole books is a feature of the biblical commentaries found at Qumran. The primitive church enlarged the range of Messianic texts to include passages which prove the disputed contention that the Messiah should suffer and die before achieving his work of salvation.[40] The most notable passage is the Suffering Servant prophecy of Isaiah 53, probably referred to in 1 Cor. 15.3 ('Christ died for our sins according to the scriptures') and quoted extensively in the New Testament. We shall see a clear allusion to Isa. 53.12 in 9.28. It is also probable in the light of the parallel in Rom. 8.34 that the notion of Christ's heavenly intercession (7.25; 9.24) is a traditional item based on the Hebrew text of Isa. 53.12 (not directly available to Hebrews, as the Greek text differs).[41]

Because Jesus is the pivot of the transition from the old age to the new, he is the focus of human aspiration as expressed in the Scriptures. So Hebrews applies to him quotations which denote solidarity with humanity in 2.12–13, citing Ps. 22.22 and Isa. 8.17–18. In 10.5–10 the situation of the psalmist in Ps. 40.6–8 is taken to be a description of the circumstances of the coming of Jesus to perform his saving work. Here, then, Jesus is the speaker in the psalm, or at least in this part of the psalm, when it is interpreted as prophecy. In this case Hebrews is encouraged to see it in this light, because it refers to an event which is fulfilled in Jesus, i.e. the preparation for the saving act of his sacrificial death and the abolition of the old sacrificial system which it entails.

The contrast between old and new raises the question whether it is correct to refer to the interpretation of Scripture in Hebrews as typology. In considering the use of Psalm 95 we saw how Hebrews argues from the theme of the promised land in the Old Testament to the future 'sabbath rest for the people of God'. However, this is not really a case of typology, because it is not a case of a repeating pattern. In the modern study of typology it is usually assumed that the Old Testament dis-

---

[40] Cf. Lindars, *New Testament Apologetic* pp. 75–137.

[41] Cf. n. 13 above. Though the allusion in Rom. 8.34 is not mentioned in many of the major commentaries on Romans (e.g. Käsemann, Cranfield), it is recognised by F. F. Bruce, *Epistle of Paul to the Romans*, Tyndale NT Commentaries (Leicester, 1963), *ad loc.*, along with other allusions to the Servant prophecies.

closes the pattern of God's saving action in history, which culminates in the act of God in Christ. This then allows the exegete to refer to the fulfilment in Christ in terms of the Old Testament type, so that one can speak of redemption by Christ as a new Exodus or of Christ himself as a new Moses. But this is not the method of Hebrews. In the case of his argument from Psalm 95 the application to the future is found within the psalm itself. Those who are addressed in the psalm belong to a much later generation, and so the warning cannot apply to the original promised land, but must refer to the future. Thus in this case Hebrews argues on the basis of what he thinks the text actually means.

Similarly the new covenant is not deduced from the Sinai covenant by the method of typological exegesis, but from the fact that it is explicitly promised in Jer. 31.31–4, quoted in 8.8–12. On the other hand Hebrews does allow his imagination to wander over some intriguing correspondences between Melchizedek and Jesus, as we shall see. That depends on the clear statement that there exists an 'order of Melchizedek' to which the Messiah is destined to belong (Ps. 110.4). That again means taking the text seriously in its literal meaning. The same thing applies to all details of sacrifice adduced from Leviticus, and to a lesser extent from Exodus, in chapters 7–10. As already mentioned, they give the definitions to which Jesus must conform for the claims made about him to be substantiated. Here, however, there is no future reference in the Old Testament text, and we have to see a different basis for the argument. It can be seen in 8.5, where the arrangements of the tent in the wilderness are said to be 'a copy and shadow of the heavenly sanctuary' on the grounds that God said to Moses, 'See that you make everything according to the pattern which was shown you on the mountain' (Exodus 25.40). This might suggest a Platonic notion, in which the literal meaning has no substance by comparison with the world of eternal forms. But this is unnecessary, because the idea that earthly temples are copies of God's heavenly dwelling was widespread in the religions of the ancient near east. Thus heaven is described as the temple in 1 *Enoch* 14 and in Revelation 4–5. What we have here, then, is analogy. The Law's definitions of sacrifice and priesthood derive their validity from the heavenly model, and Jesus must conform to them too. There is no suggestion in Hebrews that the Christian application is the only true meaning of the Old Testament. Hebrews has nothing corresponding with the allegorical interpretation of the *Epistle of Barnabas*, in which the Old Testament is treated as a code whose meaning is disclosed in Christ.[42]

Finally Hebrews' use of the Old Testament is indispensable to his purpose not only because it provides an agreed standard which his readers accept, but also because it provides the metaphorical basis for his argument. If the readers are tempted to resort to Jewish practice, the Old Testament revelation of the tent in the wilderness makes a kind of middle term in the argument between the actual temple and the actual Christ. This is one reason why his failure to mention the actual temple cannot be taken as evidence that it had ceased to exist. It is a matter of the integrity of the argument. The temple belongs to the conditions of the old covenant, and it is that which has been superseded by the establishment of the new covenant by Christ. In the same way the use of Psalm 95 in chapters 3 and 4 shows the pilgrim people in the wilderness as the middle term between the Jews and the Christians of his own day. To revert to Jewish practice is equivalent to living as if the new covenant had not yet been brought into existence.

The Holy Spirit

The Holy Spirit is mentioned only seven times in Hebrews. What little Hebrews has to say about the Spirit accords with Jewish and Christian presuppositions. But there is no empha-

---

[42] Two examples may be given. In *Barn.* 6.18–19 God's commission to men and women to rule over the fishes and birds and animals (Gen. 1.28) is recalled, and the author comments: 'Who is able now to rule over beasts or fishes or birds of heaven? ... So if this cannot be done now, surely it has been spoken for us at the time when we ourselves shall be made perfect as heirs of the covenant of the Lord.' In *Barn.* 9.8 the 318 servants of Abraham who were circumcised according to Gen. 14.14 combined with Gen. 17.23 are said to foreshadow Jesus and the cross, because the Greek numerals for ten (I) and eight (H) begin the name JEsus (*IHsous*) and 300 (T) denotes the cross.

sis on the Spirit, and in fact the Spirit plays no part in the argument of the letter. This may cause surprise to some readers, but it is not really significant. No special doctrine of the Holy Spirit had been developed and accepted universally at the time when Hebrews was written. There are two main usages.

We have already seen that when Hebrews referred to the evangelisation of his readers he used a characteristic phrase of the apostolic mission, 'by signs and wonders and various miracles and by gifts of the Holy Spirit distributed according to his own will' (2.4). Here it should be noted that the Greek text omits the definite article before 'Holy Spirit'. The same thing happens in 6.4, where our participation in Holy Spirit is mentioned along with 'the heavenly gift' and 'the goodness of the word of God and the powers of the age to come'. The description is reminiscent of the claim of Peter on the Day of Pentecost that the eschatological outpouring of the Spirit prophesied by Joel has been fulfilled (Acts 2.14–33). The omission of the article in this kind of context is normal in Luke's writings, and indeed occurs at Acts 2.4. This also happens frequently in the rest of the New Testament, and it does not seem possible to establish a consistent rule. But the oscillation between use or omission of the article is not just a matter of Greek grammar, but is due to the special character of the idea which the phrase denotes.[43]

'Spirit' (*ruaḥ*) in the Old Testament is one of those words which, when applied to God, refers to an attribute of God (in this case his power) which may be objectified as almost a separate being.[44] Thus 'the Spirit of the Lord came upon Jephthah' (Judg. 11.29), which means that God endued Jephthah with his own power. In New Testament times the

---

[43] N. Turner, *Grammatical Insights into the New Testament* (Edinburgh, 1965) attempted to establish a grammatical ruling, leading to the impossible suggestion that anarthrous 'holy spirit' is to be distinguished from the Holy Spirit as a 'divine influence possessing men' (p. 19). J. D. G. Dunn, *Baptism in the Holy Spirit* (London, 1970), p. 70, denied this, asserting that the difference was only stylistic. See the discussion in A. Jones, 'Lukan Descriptions of the Holy Spirit' (unpublished M. A. dissertation, Newcastle, NSW, 1988), 58–70.

[44] Cf. F. Baumgärtel, 'Spirit in the OT', in the article on *pneuma* in *TDNT*, VI, pp. 359–68.

word was widely used to denote angelic spirits, and so the phrase 'the Holy Spirit', which occurs only three times in the Old Testament, tended to be used in contexts where 'Spirit' alone might be misleading, to ensure that it was clear that the Spirit of God was intended. But it continued to be a fluid idea, the power of God as an active force, and it is a mistake to apply to it the later dogmatic definitions of the personality of the Spirit which belong to trinitarian theology. The omission of the definite article helps to preserve the notion of divine influence when the context is concerned with the spirit's gifts. On the other hand the article is usually retained when the emphasis falls on the Spirit as the active agent of God's power. In 10.29, where the Greek includes the article, 'the Spirit of grace' refers to the Spirit as the giver of gifts which flow from the grace of God.[45]

In the second main usage of 'the Holy Spirit' the article is always used. This comes in the introduction to biblical quotations, implying that the real author is the Holy Spirit (3.7; 9.8; 10.15). The first case is interesting, because Hebrews recognises that the human author is David (4.7). In New Testament times the Holy Spirit is frequently referred to as the source of prophetic inspiration, and this lies behind the tendency to think of the Scriptures almost as a divine oracle, which is characteristic of Alexandrian interpretation.

The only other reference to the Holy Spirit is disputed. Hebrews 9.14 speaks of Christ 'who through the eternal Spirit offered himself without blemish to God'. The phrase has frequently been interpreted to mean 'in his divine nature'.[46] But this depends on considerations derived from later dogmatic christology, and Hebrews nowhere contrasts Jesus'

---

[45] The unusual phrase is due to the fact that Hebrews here makes deliberate allusion to the promise of an outpouring of the spirit of grace (LXX; RSV 'of compassion') in Zech. 12.10. The connection is particularly interesting in relation to Hebrews' use of Scripture, for the same verse refers to the people as 'looking on him whom they have pierced' (quoted in John 19.37 and Rev. 1.7) and mourning for him (cf. Matt. 24.30; Rev. 1.7), and leads up to the promise of a fountain 'to cleanse them from sin and uncleanness' (Zech. 13.1). This shows how much of the use of Scripture in Hebrews is built on a tradition of exegesis, which he extends for the purpose of his argument.

[46] Braun, p. 269, gives a long list of scholars who have taken this view.

spiritual nature with his human nature. In fact he is most
insistent that Jesus died as a member of the human race, and
this is essential to his highpriestly character (2.10–18). This
had just been made plain in 9.11–12, in which his function as
high priest is identified with an act involving his own blood. It
therefore seems best to follow Bruce and Wilson in taking up
the opinion of St Thomas Aquinas[47] that the phrase means 'by
the power of the Holy Spirit', which is his Messianic endowment and which empowered him to fulfil his vocation like
Jephthah and the other heroes of old. On this view 9.14 should
be classed with the first group of references to the Holy Spirit.

THE PRIESTHOOD OF JESUS (1): NECESSITY OF MATURE UNDERSTANDING

In our understanding of the idea of perfection and contrast of
the old and the new in the theology of Hebrews we have seen
how the warnings to the readers have increased in severity
from the mild rebuke in 2.1–4 through stronger exhortations in
3.12 and 4.1 to the stern warning of 4.11–13. At the same time
Hebrews has been careful to soften the harshness of his words
by stressing the mercy and compassion of Jesus. This feature is
closely connected with the theme of priesthood, which has been
introduced as a metaphor in 2.17. So the same theme is picked
up once more in 4.14–16 to offset the harshness of the warning,
and by this means it is ready to be tackled in earnest in the
chapters which follow.

The theme of priesthood is introduced with a preliminary
statement in 5.1–10, and this is the first place where it is made
clear that the theme is not just a metaphor but is meant
seriously. Jesus really is a high priest. But before going into
details Hebrews interrupts the argument by insisting on the
necessity of mature understanding (5.11–14), and then an even
more terrifying warning followed, by even more appealing

---

[47] Quoted by Spicq, II, p. 258. In spite of praising the commentary of St Thomas
Aquinas most highly in general, Spicq here accepts the divine nature, adducing
7.16, 24 in favour of it (but it is doubtful if these verses refer specifically to the divine
nature either!).

reassurances, which occupy the whole of chapter 6, so that the real argument does not begin until chapter 7. From there it is continued without a break until its conclusion in 10.18. Then there is another summary of the idea of Jesus's priesthood, comparable to 4.14–16, followed by a very stern warning, comparable to 6.4–6. These conjunctions of the priesthood theme and dire threats, both growing in intensity and fullness as the letter moves forward, and finally encapsulating the argument of 7.1–10.18, give the strongest indication that the priestly work of Jesus is the heart of our author's doctrine and the crucial issue in the situation which he is trying to remedy.

According to my reconstruction of the situation of the readers the real problem is that their confidence has been undermined by their consciousness of sin (9.9, 14; 10.2). The sense of sin inevitably creates a barrier between them and God, interfering with the direct access to God established by the saving death of Christ. There is no need to doubt that at their conversion these Christians had accepted the gospel that at his death Jesus 'had made purification for sins' (1.3). That was all right for their past sins. But now that they have a growing sense of the accumulation of post-baptismal sins, they are worried because their new way of life does not give them anything practical to do in order to put it right, unlike their Jewish past.[48] It is for this reason that they are seeking solace in reversion to Jewish purification rites and return to the Jewish community for the sake of solidarity with the sacrificial system of the temple in Jerusalem, however far away it may have been. They are under pressure from their Jewish friends to abandon their Christian allegiance altogether.

In this situation it is essential for Hebrews to deal with the group both at the level of conscience and from the point of view of practice. They must be persuaded that, though the sacrifice of Jesus is unrepeatable, it continues to be effective to cope with their present consciousness of sin, and that there is a practical way of maintaining the sense of unhindered relationship with

---

[48] This reflects a well-known psychological need, experienced by all normal people, to do something practical to make amends when relationships are broken by sin and guilt. See further below, pp. 85–9, 117, 134.

God. To achieve this purpose it is not enough to repeat the standard teaching which they have already received. Presumably the leaders have already done that without success. It is necessary to produce a fresh argument, specially tailored to fit the actual situation. It must show the insufficiency of the Jewish customs, so as to prevent the 'drift' (2.1) from the original message to a compromise position which threatens to end in apostasy. It must also show in detail how the sacrifice of Christ applies in the present to meet their need. Thus Hebrews is conscious that he is giving a new exposition of the sacrifice of Christ. It is a mistake to suppose that it is a repetition of teaching previously given. It is on the contrary a creative, new development of the original teaching, a striking and original presentation of the kerygma that 'Christ died for our sins according to the scriptures' (1 Cor. 15.3).

This is the reason why Hebrews demands a special effort of understanding on the part of his readers. He has got to overcome their resistance and secure their close attention to an argument which is aimed at opening their eyes to facets of the kerygma which they have not previously realised. Moreover it is the hope of Hebrews that they will be completely convinced by what he has to say and will change their behaviour accordingly. It is no easy task.

The way in which he does this is first to give a brief statement of the basis of the argument in the real (not metaphorical) priesthood of Jesus, then to call for mature understanding, followed by the strongest possible warning of the danger of apostasy, and finally to renew rapport with the readers with positive assurances, composed in such a way as to lead back to the main subject of priesthood.

The priesthood of Jesus the Messiah

The statement of 5.1–10 adds a new dimension to the traditional christology, which we considered in a previous section. Hebrews is going to argue that everything that belongs to the Jewish sacrificial system for removing the barrier of sin has been done by Jesus in a way that makes access to God

permanent in spite of the 'sin which clings so closely' (12.1).[49]
He thoroughly understands that sins are bound to occur, and
that is why he is so insistent on the compassionate nature of
Jesus as high priest. This point is important, because the
harsh words of 6.4–6 have given Hebrews a bad reputation as
a puritanical rigorist which is wholly unwarranted. It is his
pastoral understanding of the delicate consciences of his
readers which has provided the opening for the metaphor of
priesthood in the first place. He now says that it is a proper
characteristic of a high priest to exercise this kind of compassionate concern. It is thus the primary datum in the claim
that Jesus is a real high priest. This is then confirmed by a
demonstration of the fact that Jesus was actually appointed
by God himself as a high priest.

Perhaps because this is intended as a programmatic statement, 5.1–10 is constructed in the form of a chiasmus:[50]

a A priest is commissioned to 'deal gently' with sinners (1–2).
b His ministry is on behalf of all people, including himself (3).
c It is a divinely called status (4).
c' Jesus was divinely called (5–6).
b' Jesus shared our sufferings and learnt the meaning of human
obedience (7–8).
a' Jesus thus became the means of salvation to all in his priestly
capacity (9–10).

Several features of this statement call for comment. First
Hebrews prefers to refer to the high priest, and to call Jesus
high priest, although only 'priest' is used in the crucial quotation of Ps. 110.4 in verse 6. This is not because there is any
fundamental distinction between them. Hebrews can quite
happily refer to Jesus as priest as well (cf. 7.15–16). But in the
subsequent exposition he will base his argument on the ceremonial of the Day of Atonement, which is performed by the

---

[49] 'Clings so closely' translates *euperistaton*, a rare word of doubtful meaning. But the
basic meaning must be 'easily surrounding' (so MM), so that in theory it could have
either a good or a bad sense (bad here, of course). The difficulty may explain the
early variant in P[46], *euperispaston* = 'easily distracting' (used by Paul in 1 Cor. 7.35),
but that gives the wrong meaning.
[50] Westcott, p. 121.

high priest alone, and it is necessary to show that what Jesus
has done is superior to this.

Secondly the emphasis on the pastoral character of the
priestly office is calculated to be specially appealing to the
readers in their troubled plight. The idea is applied to several
notable high priests in the contemporary Jewish literature (for
example 2 Macc. 15.12; Josephus, *Ant.* xi.318–19, 326).[51]
These were admired in contrast with the high priests of
Hebrews' own day, who were appointed on political grounds
and often behaved outrageously. But of course the model for
both Hebrews and these Jewish writers is the standard implied
by the duties assigned to the priests in the Law. For in
performing the sacrifices they act on behalf of the worshippers
and so minister to their needs. The sin offerings and guilt
offerings are provided specially for obtaining forgiveness and
reconciliation with God. Moreover the Law provides that on
the Day of Atonement the high priest should offer a sacrifice for
his own sins separately from the sacrifice for the people as a
whole (5.3; cf. Lev. 16.11, 15). Thus in theory the high priest
shares the experience of the need for forgiveness which everyone feels – including, of course, the readers.

However, there can be little doubt that Hebrews also has in
mind the pastoral ministry of Jesus. It is widely held that in
verse 7 there is allusion to the Gethsemane tradition (Mark
14.32–42 and parallels). It has already been asserted in
connection with the humanity of Jesus that 'he himself has
suffered and been tempted' (2.18). This has been recalled as a
pastoral qualification for the priesthood in 4.15: 'One who in
every respect has been tempted as we are, yet without sinning.'
In 5.8 the point is made in such a way as to make Jesus the
model for the readers. He 'learned obedience through what he
suffered' and so can save 'all who obey him' (verse 9). The
readers too need to learn obedience through their sufferings
and temptations.

But in what sense can it be said that Jesus was tempted

---

[51] Cf. R. A. Stewart, 'The Sinless High Priest', *NTS*, 14 (1967–8), 126–35; W.
Horbury, 'The Aaronic Priesthood in the Epistle to the Hebrews', *JSNT*, 19 (1983),
43–71, especially 59–66.

'without sinning' (4.15), 'was heard for his godly fear' (5.7), and 'learned obedience' (5.8)? These phrases have been chosen for their application to the readers. But they still demand explanation. In fact the Gethsemane tradition is sufficient answer, though some allusion to the temptations narrative (Matt. 4.1–11) is not excluded. The crucial issue at Gethsemane was that Jesus overcame his human shrinking from suffering by submitting himself to the will of God as Father. Thus he was tempted without sinning on this decisive occasion. Hebrews (like countless theologians ever afterwards) has generalised it to apply to the whole of his life. His 'godly fear' (the same word as 'reverence' in 12.28) is best understood as a further reference to his submission to the Father's will, which made his sacrifice acceptable (cf. 10.10).[52] For the death of Jesus could not be interpreted as a sacrifice if he did not have the intention of making it so. Similarly the inner struggle at Gethsemane can be described as 'learning obedience'. In spite of his exalted status as Son of God (just mentioned in 5.5), he was not exempt from this human experience.[53]

Thirdly, besides these pastoral qualifications, which need not mean anything more than the metaphor of priesthood, Jesus was actually appointed high priest by God, so that his priesthood is real. This is explained in 5.5–6, where Hebrews first states the Messiahship of Jesus, making him Son of God,

[52] Some editors (e.g. Harnack, Montefiore) think that this means that Jesus' prayer was heard so that he was saved from his anxiety (literally 'heard from anxiety' as an alternative to 'heard from godly fear', cf. BAG, s.v. *eulabeia*). But the context requires that he was 'heard' in the sense that, having submitted to God's will, he was enabled by God to go through death to exaltation, as indicated in verses 8–9; cf. Wilson, pp. 98–100.

[53] Another factor making for the idea of the sinlessness of Jesus was the claim that he was innocent of the charges brought against him at his trials, so that he was wrongfully condemned, and this was seen to accord with the prophecy of Isa. 53.7–9. From this point of view he was 'a lamb without blemish' (1 Pet. 1.19; cf. 2.22), a tradition which is taken up in Heb. 9.14. Moreover, in claiming that Jesus is a real high priest, Hebrews must show him to be ceremonially pure to perform his sacrificial function: cf. 8.26 (for possible references to the moral sinlessness of high priests in Jewish sources see Stewart, 'The Sinless High-Priest', 126–35). The NT does not argue that Jesus was incapable of sin on account of his divine nature (which would be ruinous to Hebrews' argument), nor need we suppose that he never did anything wrong throughout his human life. The point is that he was without sin in any respects which would have disqualified him for his God-given task of reconciling humanity and God.

by repeating the quotation of Ps. 2.7 which he had used in 1.5, and then quotes Ps. 110.4, which proves that the Messiah is appointed by God 'a priest for ever after the order of Melchizedek'. Though Ps. 110.1 was widely used as a Messianic psalm, there is no evidence that anyone had thought of exploiting this verse before. It is so important for the purpose of Hebrews, besides being an innovation, that he only states it now, and makes his strong appeal for maturity of understanding before beginning to build his argument on it in chapter 7.

It is my view that Hebrews arrived at this position entirely as a response to the need to find a convincing argument for the benefit of his readers. But we must take into account that in the previous century there had been a line of priest-kings in the Hasmonean dynasty in Judaea, and that some Jews (notably the Qumran Sect) looked forward to the appearance of two Messiahs, the priestly Messiah of Aaron and the royal Messiah of Israel. These possible influences are relevant only if they contribute to explaining what Hebrews says. But this does not seem to be the case. The Hasmonean rulers were Levites, descendants of Simon, who had accepted the position of high priest after the death of his brother Jonathan in 141 BC. They were both brothers of Judas Maccabeus, who led the Maccabean Revolt in 167 BC. By the time that Simon took over, political independence had been won, and by formal decree he was made 'leader and high priest for ever' (1 Macc. 14.41). This means that the position is to be hereditary, but not really in perpetuity, as it is only 'until a trustworthy prophet should arise'. It is uncertain whether there is any literary allusion to Ps. 110.4 in these words.[54] Though Simon's successors later took the style 'king', they were not descendants of David, and Davidic Messianism sprang into prominence in this period

---

[54] Recent commentaries on 1 Maccabees do not recognise the allusion, which can be accepted only if 'leader' (*hēgoumenon*) is intended to be Messianic and 'high priest' is a deliberate substitute for 'priest', as is the case in Hebrews, as 'for ever' (*eis ton aiōna*) is not enough to secure the literary link. If there really is allusion to Ps. 110.4, it is most likely to arise from the use of this psalm in the liturgy of installation of the high priest, in which this originally royal psalm is applied to the high priest along with the transference of robes and functions formerly belonging to the king in old Israel. But whether it was so used is unknown.

partly as a matter of protest against them.[55] It is difficult to see any way in which Hebrews might have used them as a model for his christology.

The Qumran Sect apparently did not accept the high-priesthood of the Hasmoneans and awaited the restoration of the legitimate high priest of the family of Zadok and the legitimate king of the house of David.[56] The *Damascus Document* regularly refers to 'the Messiah of Aaron and Israel', but there is no indication elsewhere in the Scrolls that a single person was expected to fulfil both roles.[57] But if the *Damascus Document* does mean one person, it must be the priestly Messiah, as Aaron is always mentioned first and in 14.19 he is apparently to make atonement for the iniquity of the people.[58] In this case he has acquired the title of the royal Messiah too, exactly the opposite of what we have in Hebrews. In fact Hebrews shows no awareness of the expectation of a priestly Messiah. He is not saying that one man combines the function of two Messiahs. But he has found a text which says that the Messiah is himself a

[55] Aristobulus I (reigned 104–103 BC) is said by Josephus (*Ant.* XIII. 320) to be the first of the Hasmonean high priests to adopt the title 'king', but his coins do not bear this out. However, his successor Alexander Jannaeus (103–76 BC) certainly took the title, and it was used by the remaining Hasmonean rulers. The *Psalms of Solomon*, composed about 50 BC, are deeply opposed to the Hasmoneans and express the popular longing for a righteous king (called *Christos*, i.e. Messiah, in the Greek text) of the house of David.

[56] 1QS 9.11 speaks of the coming of 'the Prophet and the Messiahs of Aaron and Israel', and 1QSᵃ legislates for the conduct of the community when the two Messiahs are present, the Priest-Messiah taking precedence over the Messiah of Israel, as in most other texts. The application of 'Messiah' to the high priest probably stems from the Babylonian Exile, when the monarchy ceased and the high priest took over his liturgical functions. In the restoration Zechariah 3–6 expects a partnership of two Messiahs, priest and king. But this hope was disappointed, and the high priest remained sole native leader during the period of Persian and Greek rule.

[57] CD, known from the Cairo Genizah texts before the discovery of the Dead Sea Scrolls, is perhaps to be classed with *Jubilees* and 11QTemple as an Essene work separate from the books specifically emanating from the community at Qumran. But fragments have been found in the Qumran caves, and these confirm the singular 'Messiah' in the references.

[58] The text is fragmentary at this point and the interpretation is uncertain. Lohse (*Die Texte aus Qumran* (Munich, 1984), p. 97) and Vermes (*The Dead Sea Scrolls in English*, 3rd edn (London, 1987), p. 99) both take the verb as active (piel) with 'the Messiah' as subject, but it could be passive (pual) with 'their iniquity' as subject. If so, the coming of the Messiah marks the time when the need for atonement is complete.

priest, and that is what he needs for his argument. Hebrews, like Paul (Rom. 1.3), knows that Jesus was descended from the royal tribe of Judah (7.14).

Mature understanding

Because the subject of Christ's priesthood is new, Hebrews seeks to win the attention of his readers by appealing to their self-esteem. They would not like to be regarded as children who are not old enough to know the difference between good and bad.[59] So he presents the subject as more advanced teaching, which is necessary for those who wish to 'go on to maturity [*teleiotēs*, literally perfection]'.[60] They have already received basic teaching, which was good enough to start with, but has proved to be insufficient in the present situation. What they need now is complete understanding of the implications of the 'elementary doctrines of Christ' which they have previously learnt (6.1).

The list of these foundation-beliefs, however, is strange. They have received 'a foundation of repentance from dead works and of faith toward God, with instruction[61] about ablutions (*baptismōn*), the laying on of hands, the resurrection of the dead, and eternal judgment' (6.1–2). There is nothing specifically Christian about this list, which could easily be a summary of Jewish doctrines and practice, especially as the word for 'ablutions' is not the usual word for Christian baptism but refers to Jewish washings in 9.10 and in Mark 7.4, which are the only other places where the word occurs in the New Testament. This one difficult word is decisive for many

---

[59] There is dispute about the exact meaning of 'unskilled in the word of righteousness' (5.13), but the context shows that it is intended to be the opposite of 'trained by practice to distinguish good from evil' (verse 14), so that it means 'unskilled in the subject of morality'.

[60] Thus *teleiotēs* here means 'complete understanding'. Hebrews is not suggesting that the readers are really incapable of taking the 'solid food' of his teaching, but wishes to sting them into being willing to make the effort to give it full attention.

[61] RSV rightly takes 'instruction' as accusative (*didachēn*) in apposition to 'foundation', following P46 and B, against the genitive (*didachēs*) found in the vast majority of manuscripts and adopted in recent editions of the Greek New Testament (UBS and Nestle–Aland). Thus four items of teaching are specified which accompany conversion as a result of repentance and faith.

commentators. Thus Spicq, Bruce, and Buchanan think of the continuation of such Jewish practices in the Christian community. Nairne even suggests that the author is referring to the attempt to reintroduce specifically Jewish practices on the part of the readers, who thereby put themselves in an 'impossible' position (6.4). Montefiore, assuming the authorship of Apollos, applies the plural to two sorts of baptism, that of John the Baptist and that of the church. Westcott suggests various unspecified Christian lustrations including baptism. But, as with the eucharist (see above, pp. 9–12), we have to remember Hebrews' allusive style. He is not giving a formal catalogue, but a general suggestion of basic practices (ablutions and laying on of hands) and doctrines (general resurrection and judgment). Baptism and the laying on of hands go together in Acts 19.5–6. The non-technical word is used in the plural to suggest individual acts of baptism, which is accompanied by the laying on of hands in each case. It is of course impossible to determine from this one reference the significance of the laying on of hands in the Hebrews church and how it relates to the information in Acts and the Pastoral Epistles.[62]

That Hebrews does mean Christian initiation, with repentance and faith as the basic dispositions for baptism, and resurrection and judgment as its eschatological reference, is suggested by the warning which follows in 6.4–5. For here the process of initiation is described in glowing terms, intended to remind the readers of the inspiring character of their own baptism. Their minds were 'enlightened' by the teaching which culminated in the act of baptism.[63] They 'tasted the

---

[62] In Acts the laying on of hands follows baptism, apparently as part of the initiation, in Acts 8.17; 19.6, but it is also used for the commissioning of missionaries (Acts 13.3) and of officers in the church (Acts 6.6). It is also used in the healing of the sick (Acts 9.17) as in the Gospels, but that is unlikely to be the meaning here. In 1 Tim. 4.14; 5.22; 2 Tim. 1.6 it refers to ordination. Apart from the use in healing (which in biblical and rabbinic references employs a different Hebrew verb), the rest are all facets of empowering with the Holy Spirit for different purposes, and this is probably what is meant here. See D. Daube, *The New Testament and Rabbinic Judaism* (London, 1956), pp. 224–46.

[63] 'Enlightened' is used again of Christian initiation in 10.32, and later became a technical term for being baptised (so the Syriac Peshitta here, and cf. Justin, 1 *Ap.* 61.12–13; 65.1). Here it refers to the reception of the gospel more generally, and is comparable to (but not dependent on) the use of the idea of illumination in the

heavenly gift' and became 'partakers of the Holy Spirit' through their incorporation into Christ (cf. 2.4). Thereby they 'tasted the goodness of the word of God', declared in the gospel, and experienced already 'the powers of the age to come'. In this way the readers received an excellent foundation on which the complete understanding, which they now require, can be built.

Impossibility of reconciliation?

In the present situation, however, all this is in danger of being lost. Reversion to Jewish purification practices implies denial of this splendid foundation of faith, and in the actual circumstances carries with it the real risk of apostasy. Hebrews must show that he is well aware of this danger. Hitherto his warnings have been gentle, aimed at retaining the goodwill of the readers. But it is essential to make it clear that he knows the real position, if they are to take what he has to say seriously.

This is what he does in 6.4–12. First he shows the dire consequences of apostasy (4–6), adding an agricultural metaphor to suggest the divine judgment (7–8). Then he changes his tune and assures the readers that he knows that they have not actually committed apostasy, urging them to recall their first zeal and to maintain it to the end (9–12). These two contradictory suggestions enhance the impression that the danger of apostasy is real and that Hebrews is trying to pull them back from the brink.

This must be borne in mind as we tackle the apparent rigorism of 6.4–6.[64] These verses have caused misery to people

mystery religions. The Christian use may well be derived from Ps. 34.5 (RSV 'be radiant'), where the LXX uses the same Greek word. The same psalm also provides 'tasted' as another image for reception of the gospel (Ps. 34.8, quoted in a baptismal context in 1 Pet. 2.5), and may well have been recited liturgically at baptisms. This suggests further that the 'tasting' may have been applied to the eucharist following initiation, which seals the experience of 'the kindness of the Lord', or as Hebrews says, 'the goodness of the word of God', made possible through incorporation into Christ.

[64] For the interpretation of these verses see R. C. Sauer, 'A Critical and Exegetical Reexamination of Hebrews 5:11 to 6:8' (unpublished Ph.D dissertation, Manchester, 1981).

of scrupulous conscience for centuries, because they have been applied not merely to apostasy, which is the clear meaning in the context, but to grave sin of any kind. Some have applied them to the 'sin against the Holy Spirit' (Mark 3.29), or to the idea of mortal sin in 1 John 5.16. Tertullian, writing soon after AD 220, quotes 6.4–8 in full to rebut the suggestion that a 'second repentance' is available for adulterers. For, he says, 'he who learnt from the apostles and taught with the apostles [cf. 2.3] never knew any second repentance promised by the apostles to the adulterer and fornicator' (*On Modesty* 20). The insistence of Hebrews that Jesus is a merciful high priest (4.14–16) shows conclusively that this is the wrong track.

The apostasy of the readers, if it were to happen, would make renewal to repentance impossible. We must remember that, though Hebrews writes in general terms, he is thinking of the actual readers who are seeking for a remedy for their consciousness of sin. Paradoxically they are turning away from the means of reconciliation in the endeavour to find it. This is suggested by verse 6b, where the present participles translated 'crucify'[65] and 'hold up to contempt' refer to a continuing situation resulting from the act of apostasy. It means repudiation of the basic faith that Jesus is the Son of God whose death has procured purification of sins (1.1–4). This point becomes clearer in the light of the comparable stern warning in 10.26, 29, where we are told that 'if we sin deliberately after receiving the knowledge of the truth, there no longer remains a sacrifice for sins' for one 'who has spurned the Son of God, and profaned the blood of the covenant by which he was sanctified, and outraged the Spirit of grace'. The deliberate sin referred to here is of course apostasy. It leaves 'no chance to repent' (12.17), because the reconciliation, which is a permanent effect of the establishing of the covenant through the sacrifice of Christ, has

---

65 Older translations (AV, RV) follow the Greek Fathers, who take the word *anastaurountas* to mean 'crucify afresh', against the normal meaning of the Greek (= 'lift up on a stake'). But Spicq, Braun, and most recent commentators accept the latter meaning as not only more correct, but also more suitable to the context. It is not that those who commit apostasy thereby crucify Jesus a second time, but that they put themselves in the position of those who actually crucified him in the first place.

been thrown away. Only by turning back to Christ would renewal be possible.

Controversy rages over the interpretation of these verses. The idea that the impossibility of renewal applies only so long as the readers refuse to turn back to Christ is dismissed as a truism.[66] Usually it is claimed that Hebrews means a psychological impossibility on the grounds that those who have experienced the blessings of the life of faith and then repudiated them are harder to reclaim than those who have never previously experienced them (so Westcott, supported by Bruce). But it is not necessary to suppose that Hebrews is arguing a general and theoretical case at all. He is speaking to readers who, he fears, are about to take an irrevocable step. What he would say to them if they did take it and then subsequently sought reconciliation we cannot say. But I suspect that, in spite of what he says here, he would welcome them with open arms! It is unsound to assume that in a work of such marked rhetorical character the writer should never allow himself some element of exaggeration. Here he immediately softens the extreme severity of his words by the gentler device of the metaphor of fruitful and unfruitful soil (6.7–8). He then has another device – equally exaggerated – when in verse 9 he makes a *captatio benevolentiae*[67] expressing his *assurance* that such a case does not apply to the readers, here called 'beloved' for the only time in the whole epistle. Of course he knows it does! It is precisely what he is most afraid of.

Hebrews is well aware of the danger of an overkill. This is why in verse 9 he denies any suggestion that the readers have actually gone so far as to commit apostasy. Their former good works are commended, and they are told not to be 'sluggish' (verse 12). But it is obvious that he really fears that they might go overboard any time, and we should not be fooled, like so many commentators, into thinking that he *only* means slackness. In commending as the alternative 'faith and patience', he

---

[66] Bruce, p. 124: 'A truism hardly worth putting into words.'

[67] I.e. 'capturing the goodwill' of the readers by means of a delicate compliment. Paul uses this rhetorical device in 1 Cor. 11.2 and elsewhere: cf. E. Schüssler Fiorenza, 'Rhetorical Situation and Historical Reconstruction in 1 Corinthians', *NTS*, 33 (1987), 386–403 (on this point, p. 395).

is paving the way for the practical solution to the problem of the readers, as we shall see when we reach consideration of chapters 10–12.

Grounds for hope

However, Christian assurance does not depend on good works, but on the promises of God himself. Like Paul, Hebrews appeals to the promises made to Abraham to show that God's purpose is irrevocable.[68] Thus the promise to Abraham in Gen. 22.16–17 gives double assurance, firstly on the grounds that an oath is normally held to be reliable, and secondly because God swore by himself, who cannot lie. Continuing his policy of winning the goodwill of his readers at this point, Hebrews then gives three quick metaphors for the hope which such an assured promise engenders. It is like a place of refuge for those in need. It is like an anchor in rough seas. It is like admission beyond the veil of the sanctuary which is the place of the presence of God himself.

This last metaphor brings the subject back to the priesthood of Jesus. Entry beyond the veil symbolises direct access to God which belongs to the eschatological age. It is available already through Jesus, because in his priestly act of sacrifice he has passed beyond the veil as our 'forerunner' (*prodromos* = the advance party in a military campaign), which is another way of referring to him as the 'pioneer' (2.10). Direct access to God requires the removal of the barrier of sin. Jesus has done this because he is 'a high priest for ever after the order of Melchizedek' (6.20). The readers should now be alert and ready to give full attention to Hebrews' exposition of this crucial doctrine.

THE PRIESTHOOD OF JESUS (2): THE MEDIATOR OF THE NEW COVENANT

The main argument of Hebrews on the sacrifice of Christ, which we shall now consider in this and in the following section, has three principal strands which are all equally

---

[68] For Paul see Gal. 3.6–9; Rom. 4 and 11.29.

necessary. The first, already enunciated in 5.1–10, is the real priesthood of the Messiah, which qualifies him to perform the sacrifice which is required for atonement for sins. This is a special kind of priesthood, the order of Melchizedek, and it is essential to achieve the object of procuring permanent efficacy, unlike the sacrifices of the Levitical priesthood. The second strand is the eschatological concept of the inauguration of the new covenant. This is what gives to Christ's sacrifice its permanent efficacy, because it opens the era of salvation in which fresh sacrifices for sin are no longer required. The third strand is the model of the Day of Atonement, which provides the essential requirements for an atoning sacrifice. It is shown that these are fulfilled in the sacrificial death of Jesus, so that it cannot be objected that there is no remedy available to the readers in their troubled state of consciousness of sin. These three strands are woven together with superb skill to make a compelling argument for the sufficiency of the sacrifice of Christ as atonement for sins for all time.

The order of Melchizedek

The reference to Melchizedek in Ps. 110.4 is made without any explanation. It can be assumed that the psalmist regarded it as self-explanatory. The only other place in the Old Testament where Melchizedek is mentioned is Gen. 14.18–20. This is a strange episode (thought by some scholars to be an interpolation) in the story of the slaughter of kings, in which Abraham (still called Abram at this stage in Genesis) rescues his nephew Lot. For no apparent reason Melchizedek king of Salem (i.e. Jerusalem) appears, bringing bread and wine, and blesses Abram by God Most High, and Abram gives him a tenth of the spoils. It has been conjectured that the tradition arose in connection with David's capture of Jerusalem from the Jebusites (2 Sam. 5.6–7). The 'zedek' component (= righteousness) may have been the name or title of the Jebusite god. We suddenly find in 2 Sam. 8.17 that David has a court priest called Zadok, who is the ancestor of the Zadokite priests from whom the high priest was appointed until the highpriesthood passed to the Hasmoneans. Though given a genealogy going back through Eleazar to Aaron in 1 Chr. 6.8, it is possible that he was the deposed priest-king of Jerusalem and that the use of 'God Most High' as a title for Yahweh, which is especially frequent in the Zion psalms, is one facet of David's adoption of the royal style of the Jebusite kings. If so, Ps. 110.4 may preserve the memory of the investiture of David or his successors as priest-king. The insertion of Gen. 14.18–20 into its context has been thought to represent the legitimation of David's collection of tribute from all the tribes of Israel after establishing himself in Jerusalem.[69]

Of course Hebrews had no knowledge of such speculations. But other writers of his time were interested in the figure of Melchizedek, and we must see whether he owes a debt to them. There is, firstly, good reason to suppose that he knew some of the ideas used by Philo in connection with Melchizedek, even if he was not directly dependent on Philo's writings. In the *Allegory of the Laws* III. 79 Philo sets out to expound Genesis 14 and equates Melchizedek allegorically with reason, which is the ruler of the passions. This idea is completely foreign to Hebrews, but he shares with Philo the elucidation of the names Melchizedek ('king of righteousness') and king of Salem ('king of peace'), which depends on a knowledge of the Hebrew language which Philo probably did not have (7.2). Moreover the idea in verse 3 that Melchizedek is 'without father or mother or genealogy' is based on a rabbinic principle of interpretation which is used elsewhere by Philo and is known from later Jewish sources. It is a deduction which is based on the principle that what is not mentioned in Scripture can be assumed not to have existed.[70] As this also covers the claim that he 'has neither beginning of days nor end of life', it is possible to see this as a characteristic of the 'order' of Melchizedek to which, according to Ps. 110.4, the Messiah/Son of

---

[69] Cf. G. von Rad, *Genesis: A Commentary* (London, 1961), pp. 174–6; R. de Vaux, *Ancient Israel: Its Life and Institutions* (London, 1961), pp. 310, 374.

[70] For the principle see Bruce, p. 136, n. 18. Philo uses *amētōr* ('without mother') of Sarah on the same principle (*de Ebr.* 61), but not the other words. Classical usage suggests the possibility that angelic origin is meant as opposed to human parentage, but Hebrews clearly has in mind divine origin in line with his christology.

God belongs. For he is there said to be a priest who continues *for ever*. Thus Hebrews is interested in these details not merely for their typological correspondences but because they permit him to establish a fundamentally important point in his argument concerning the priesthood of Jesus. More will have to be said about this later.

Here we must digress to point out that Hebrews is not intending to make a historical statement about Melchizedek. Many readers of Hebrews find the description in 7.1–3 quite unnerving, because it seems to make Melchizedek the eternal Son of God revealed before his time. However, although Hebrews certainly thought of him as a historical person, he is interested in him only from the point of view of the value of the text of Gen. 14.18–20 for establishing the model implied by Ps. 110.4. If the text is regarded as having a prophetic purpose, it can reveal God's intentions as much by its silences as by its positive statements. It remains true that Hebrews is dazzled by what he is able to find in this text, and knows that it is likely to make an equally impressive appeal to his readers (see verse 4).

A second possible influence on Hebrews is suggested by 11QMelchizedek, a document discovered at Qumran Cave 11 and first published in 1965.[71] This is a fascinating and tantalising fragment, in which it is asserted that the coming eschatological judgment is to be performed by a representative of God who is called Melchizedek. He thus appears to be a Messianic figure. But the document, which is basically an exegesis and application of Isa. 61.1–2 and other passages, makes no allusion at all to either Gen. 14.18–20 or Ps. 110.4. On the other hand references to Ps. 82.1 support the suggestion of Milik that Melchizedek is a symbolic name for Michael, the prince of the angels, who acts for God on behalf of Israel. The verse reads literally, 'God (*elohim*) stands in the council of God (*el*): in the midst of the Gods (*elohim*) he judges.' Both *el* and *elohim* are applied to angels in the Dead Sea Scrolls. The designation 'Melchizedek' ('my king is righteousness') is matched by the coinage of *Melchiresha'* ('my king is wicked-

---

[71] English translation in G. Vermes, *The Dead Sea Scrolls in English*, 2nd edn (Harmondsworth, 1975), pp. 265–8, and 3rd edn (Sheffield, 1987), pp. 300–2.

ness') as a name for Satan in 4Q280–2. Both names probably stood originally in the much damaged 4QAmram, which describes the prince of darkness as *Melchiresha*‘, but unfortunately the names of the prince of light have not survived.[72] The use of 'Melchizedek' as a name for Michael is also found in post-biblical sources.[73]

It is evident that there is no direct connection between 11QMelchizedek and Hebrews, in spite of the fact that in both writings the Melchizedek figure has comparable eschatological functions. But in the Qumran document he is not the Messiah, does not act as a priest, and is not the mediator of the sacrifice of the new covenant. In Hebrews everything that is said about Melchizedek is derived from the two biblical passages Gen. 14.18–20 and Ps. 110.4. In 11QMelchizedek nothing is said about him on the basis of these two passages.

Further evidence of speculation about Melchizedek appears in a Gnostic document, possibly composed in the second century AD, which is included in the Nag Hammadi texts and entitled 'Melchizedek' by its modern editors. This certainly refers to Gen. 14.18–20 for the name and title ('priest of God Most High') and applies them to Jesus, but it is too dilapidated to give a coherent sense. It is quite likely that it is dependent on Hebrews.[74]

It seems, then, that though Melchizedek was the subject of some speculation in New Testament times, Hebrews has struck out a line of his own in working out the concept of an 'order' of Melchizedek to which the Messiah belongs. Because the Messiah is an eschatological figure, he is the only member of this order. We have already seen that one feature of this order is the notion that the priest continues for ever.

---

[72] For 4Q280–82 ('Melkiresha") see Vermes, *Scrolls*, 2nd edn (1975), p. 254; 3rd edn (1987), p. 161. For 4QAmram ('The Testament of Amram') see 2nd edn, pp. 260f; 3rd edn, pp. 262f.

[73] The identification of Melchizedek of Gen. 14.18–20 and Ps. 110.4 with an angel was known to Origen, probably from Jewish speculations, and was denied by Jerome, who claimed that no Jews held this opinion. It does appear, however, in mediaeval Jewish writings. See M. de Jonge and A. S. van der Woude, '11QMelchizedek and the New Testament', *NTS*, 12 (1966), pp. 301–26.

[74] Translation in J. M. Robinson (ed.), *The Nag Hammadi Library in English* (Leiden, 1977), pp. 399–403.

The main objective is to show the difference between this order of priesthood and that of the Levitical priests. Hebrews brilliantly seizes points which he can use for this purpose from the description of Abraham's encounter with Melchizedek. Not all of them are taken up in detail. Thus 'king of righteousness' and 'king of peace' suggest the vindication of God's plan and the establishing of the heavenly city of Jerusalem, but this is not spelled out.

However, the fact that Melchizedek 'is without father or mother or genealogy, and has neither beginning of days nor end of life' is important, because it shows that he 'resembles the Son of God'.[75] This might almost be a description of the Wisdom christology in 1.2–3. Jesus is Son of God both by virtue of being the one in whom the pre-existent and eternal Wisdom/Son/Word of God has been most fully expressed, and by his exalted position as the Messiah. It is obvious that Jesus alone fulfils the requirements of this description.

In the encounter with Abraham there are two significant points. In the first place Melchizedek blessed Abraham, not the reverse. On the universally accepted principle that 'the inferior is blessed by the superior' (7.7) this shows that the priesthood of Melchizedek is superior to the Levitical priesthood, which is hereditary and descended from Abraham. Secondly Abraham paid to Melchizedek a tithe of the spoils. So whereas the Levitical priests according to the Law receive tithes from the people for their maintenance, here in the person of their ancestor they have to pay them. When Hebrews says, 'One might even say that Levi himself, who receives tithes, paid tithes through Abraham' (7.9), he is not apologising for making too bold a statement, but rather claiming to put the matter in a nutshell.[76] The idea depends on the sense of solidarity of a people with their common ancestor: cf. Isa. 51.1–2.

---

[75] Note that Hebrews does not say 'resembles Jesus', but 'the Son of God', i.e. a divine being who partakes of the characteristics of divinity, including eternal existence without human generation. Thus only a person proceeding from God or raised to this status can be a member of the order of Melchizedek.

[76] So Wilson, following J. Héring, *L'Epître aux Hébreux* (Neuchâtel, 1954), p. 69; cf. Williamson, *Philo*, pp. 103–9.

Modern readers tend to be disappointed that Hebrews makes no mention of the fact that Melchizedek brought bread and wine. This was naturally seized on as a type of the eucharist by the church Fathers and is a frequent subject in mediaeval art.[77] The reason is that it is not relevant to the purpose of Hebrews, and the notion of priesthood had not yet been applied to the celebration of the eucharist. Though the eucharist was certainly a celebration of 'the Lord's death until he comes' (1 Cor. 11.26), it was not yet regarded in itself as a priestly act. The notion of priesthood in Hebrews is entirely derived from existing Jewish ideas, and this is essential for the cogency of the argument.

The eternal priesthood of Jesus

Hebrews has derived from the Melchizedek tradition the model for the Messiah as the eschatological high priest. In 7.11–28 he applies this specifically to Jesus in such a way as to underline the points which are necessary for the argument.

His first point is that the appearance of the eschatological priest makes a complete break with the Levitical priesthood, which can then be seen to have had only limited duration. Jesus, being a descendant of Judah (7.14), was not qualified for the Levitical priesthood, but he has been proved to be the eschatological priest by virtue of being the Messiah. His sacrificial death and subsequent exaltation form the turning point in God's plan of salvation. It is the act by which he 'has been made perfect for ever' (7.28), and it has put him in the position where 'he is able for all time to save those who draw near to God through him' (verse 25). It thus follows that 'perfection' (*teleiōsis*, verse 11), i.e. the completion of God's plan, could not be reached through the Levitical priesthood, because no priestly act under the old Law has ever been shown to be capable of having this permanent effect. From the point of

---

[77] Spicq, II, p. 208, gives quotations from Clement of Alexandria ('furnishing conse-crated food for a type of the eucharist', *Strom.* IV.25) and numerous church Fathers, and draws attention to the allusion to the 'spotless offering' of Melchizedek in the *Unde et memores* section of the eucharistic prayer in the ancient Roman liturgy.

view of the readers this has two important consequences. They should now realise that they are wrong to revert to Jewish practices of purification under the Law, because these belong to an inferior (verse 7) system which has now been rendered obsolete. They should also be willing to accept the fact that, in spite of not being descended from Aaron, Jesus is properly qualified as the high priest in the new era inaugurated by his death.

Secondly, it is important for the argument to show that all the ways in which the priesthood of Jesus differs from the Levitical priesthood are necessary in view of his priestly function of achieving the completion of God's plan of salvation for humanity. So Hebrews points out that the hereditary principle is no longer relevant because what is required for this purpose is 'the power of an indestructible life' (verse 16), which Jesus has as a result of his death and resurrection. Again, it can be argued that the Levitical priesthood was defective as a divine ordinance because the regulations of Exodus 28–9 and Leviticus 8–9 for the consecration of Aaron and his sons do not include the divine oath, which is a central feature of Ps. 110.4 (verses 20–1). Moreover there is no need for a succession of priests, because Jesus lives for ever, and therefore holds his priesthood permanently (verses 23–4). Similarly there is no need for new acts of atonement, because the function of offering sacrifice on behalf of the people has been taken up into a permanent condition: 'he always lives to make intercession for us' (verse 25).[78] Finally this means that the institution of the daily sacrifices is no longer required. If the readers lived far from the temple, but maintained solidarity with it through paying the temple tax, they would especially rely on the daily sacrifices. But this institution also is to be regarded as obsolete (verse 27).

Thirdly, it is not enough to concentrate on the inadequacy of the Levitical priesthood and the sacrifices under the Law. It is

[78] 'Always' (*eis to panteles*), used only here and in Luke 13.11 in the NT, can mean either 'to the completion of time', i.e. 'always', or 'to the completion of the purpose', i.e. 'absolutely' (so NEB). 'Always' (better 'for all time') seems to me preferable, because the point is that atonement is available to the readers both now and to the end.

also necessary to show how the better sacrifice of Christ is actually effective in the present. Hebrews keeps this fact before the readers by light touches as he works through the differences between the two orders of priesthood. Thus in verse 19, after pointing out that 'the law made nothing perfect', he says that in Jesus 'a better hope is introduced, through which we draw near to God'. It is significant that 'draw near' is in the present tense. This is followed up by the statement that the oath in Ps. 110.4 'makes Jesus the surety of a better covenant' (verse 22), which is the first hint of the vitally important theme of the new covenant which will be expounded in 8.6–13. Again, the application to the present is maintained by the timeless statement that Jesus 'always lives to make intercession for us' (7.25). Finally Jesus is said to be 'fitting' for us because of his abiding personal characteristics: 'holy, blameless, unstained, separated from sinners, exalted above the heavens' (verse 26). These reflect the special purity required of the high priest, who enters the most holy place, from which ordinary people are barred. But, as will be shown in 10.1–10, the holiness of Jesus is not a matter of ceremonial purity but of moral purity, which is demonstrated in his complete offering of himself, and he has access to the heavenly sanctuary of the presence of God, of which the earthly sanctuary is only a symbol.

The new covenant

All the above argument on priesthood is really only preliminary to what Hebrews actually wants to say.[79] The conclusion to which he has been leading is that we do 'have such a high priest' (8.1), which means that we do have the means of removing the barrier of sin. He is 'seated at the right hand of the Majesty in heaven, a minister in the sanctuary and the true tent which is set up not by man but by the Lord' (8.1–2). So the ground is now prepared for the vital explanation of what Jesus does in this capacity, which can solve the problem of the

---

[79] In 8.1 the 'point' (*kephalaion*) does not mean the gist or essence of what has just been said, but the conclusion to which it leads, which is a new point; cf. William Manson, *The Epistle to the Hebrews*, Baird Lecture, 1949 (London, 1951).

readers' continuing consciousness of sin. We may observe in passing that it is significant that the present position is expressed in the familiar terms of the Messianic text Ps. 110.1 (verse 1), which shows how closely Hebrews is keeping to the terms of reference of the primitive kerygma. The description of the heavenly sanctuary as the 'true tent' opens up the terms of reference of the following argument.

In fact Hebrews has a difficult task. Because of the situation of the readers he has to focus attention on the present rather than the past. But the theme of priesthood is liable to lead back to the past because (again in line with the primitive kerygma) the priestly act of sacrifice is identified with Jesus' death for our sins. He will have to insist on the pastness of this act, that it has been done once and for all, and yet at the same time show that it provides a continuing remedy for the recurring sense of guilt which troubles the readers in the present.

For this purpose Hebrews takes up another point from the kerygma, that the sacrifice of Christ constitutes the inauguration of the new covenant of the famous prophecy of Jer. 31.31–4.[80] This is quoted in full in the present context in 8.8–12, but significantly is quoted again in shorter form at the end of the argument in 10.16–17. It thus encapsulates the whole exposition of the sacrifice of Jesus which comes in between. He also refers to Jesus as 'the mediator of a new covenant' in 9.15.

It is particularly important that Hebrews resorts to the concept of the new covenant to deal with this crucial issue, which is the nub of the whole problem which has caused such havoc in the Hebrews church. For it shows that, in spite of all the originality of thought and argumentation, he is not seeking for a solution by importing ideas from outside of the Christian tradition in which he stands. Nor is he telling his readers a new

---

[80] Though in English the idea of covenant is primarily an agreement between two parties, the Sinai covenant (Exodus 19–24) is represented as imposed by God on the people, like the suzerainty treaties imposed by the Hittite emperors on their vassal kings. The covenant can thus be regarded as God's gracious gift. This is especially true of the new covenant. For the origin and history of the covenant idea in Israel, which is much disputed, see E. W. Nicholson, *God and his People: Covenant Theology in the Old Testament* (Oxford, 1986).

point of doctrine which they have not heard before. It is something that they know already, but have not appreciated in its full significance, and this is why they have not been able to see that they already possess the answer to the problem which has brought them to the verge of apostasy.

For the prophecy of a new covenant had been taken up into the ferment of eschatological expectation before the rise of Christianity and can be traced to early strands within Christianity itself. It is referred to as a fundamental concept in the *Damascus Document*, in which the origin of the sect (either the Qumran Sect or a group of Essenes closely associated with it) is described as a withdrawal to 'enter the new covenant in the land of Damascus' (CD 6.19; cf. 8.21; 20.12). In early Christianity it appears in the tradition of the eucharistic words of Jesus ('the new covenant in my blood', 1 Cor. 11.25; cf. 'my blood of the covenant', Mark 14.24). The use of the Jeremiah text in the early church is further indicated by Rom. 11.26–7, where Paul, drawing on the growing tradition of exegetical work in the Jewish and Christian dialogue, has a conflation of two quotations which are related to it in theme, Isa. 59.20–1 and Isa. 27.9. The latter reads, 'and this will be my covenant with them when I take away their sins'. This is indeed the aspect of the new covenant theme which has the greatest relevance for Hebrews. The new covenant will establish, indeed has already established through Christ, a new relationship between God and his people in which the Law as the revealed will of God will be internalised in mutual knowledge and understanding as a result of a decisive act of forgiveness on God's part.

The new covenant theme was thus available in connection with the sacrificial death of Jesus as an atonement for sins. Hebrews builds up his argument on this basis in such a way as to reach the conclusion that the sacrifice of Jesus has produced a permanent situation in which no further act of atonement is necessary (10.18). However, this does not mean that there is nothing practical for the readers to do when they are assailed by the consciousness of sin. Another aspect of the new covenant is that it suggests what this should be. This aspect, however, will not be dealt with until the exposition of the sacrificial death of Jesus has been finished.

Before beginning this exposition Hebrews underlines yet again the fact that the old sacrificial system is obsolete. But he now changes the terms of reference to prepare for the particular range of biblical material which he will need to use in order to prove his point. He will use the laws relating to the Day of Atonement to prove that the death of Jesus is rightly to be understood as a sacrifice for sins, and the account of the inauguration of the Sinai covenant to prove that it brings into effect the new covenant. So he now points out that the existing practice of sacrifice rests on laws which were enacted as part of the Sinai covenant (8.3–6). These can be seen to be no more than a temporary measure for two good reasons. The first is that they were in any case only copies of the heavenly realities. The second is that the prophecy of the new covenant necessarily renders the old one obsolete.

The first point is important, because it is essential to the argument that the methods of atonement under the Law are inadequate. But what Hebrews actually says has wider implications. Quoting Exodus 25.40, in which God says to Moses, 'See that you make everything according to the pattern which was shown you on the mountain', he describes the sacrificial regulations as 'a copy and shadow of the heavenly sanctuary' (verse 5). This has been taken by some modern scholars to be decisive evidence that Hebrews operated with a Platonic philosophy, comparable to that of Philo. For it suggests that the earthly things are material, and therefore imperfect, copies of the immaterial and eternal heavenly archetypes, and the object of the religious quest is to pass beyond the material to the eternal. Philo, in his *Life of Moses* II. 74–5, seized on Exodus 25.40 as proof of his own Platonic understanding of revealed truth, for it suggested to him that the tent and its furnishings were copies of the archetypes which God had impressed on the mind of Moses. However, as Barrett has shown, Hebrews does not operate with these categories of thought.[81] The idea of the heavenly sanctuary is intended seriously. It carries forward the

[81] Barrett, 'Eschatology' (n. 31 above).

ancient and long-lasting idea that earthly temples are counter-parts of the actual dwellings of the gods in heaven, and it is in this sense that they can be called copies and shadows of the heavenly. We only have to look at 1 *Enoch* 14 and Revelation 4–5 to see Jewish and Jewish–Christian examples of this which bear no relation to Greek philosophy. But whereas this concept of the relationship between earthly and heavenly is essentially timeless, the Jewish eschatology shared by Hebrews sets a limit on the duration of the earthly, which is due to be superseded by the heavenly (cf. Rev. 21.1–22.5). Thus the pattern which Moses saw in vision was the heavenly reality which endures, while the arrangements of the earthly sanctuary, be it tent or temple, are due to pass away with the inauguration of the new covenant, and this is what has been achieved through the sacrifice of Jesus.[82]

The second point reinforces the first. The prophecy of the new covenant refers to a future act, in which the Sinai covenant will cease to be applicable. It thus points to an eschatological event. The contrast between the conditions of the two coven-ants proves conclusively that the old covenant was destined to become obsolete (8.13).

No doubt the readers had grasped this point when they were converted to Christian faith, as it seems to be a fundamental position of the Hebrews church. But it is not the only possible interpretation of the new covenant prophecy. The *Damascus Document* does not think of the new covenant as abrogating the Sinai covenant but as carrying it forward for a more faithful observance of it according to the precepts of the Teacher of Righteousness. In general Jews in New Testament times felt themselves to be the covenant people, and this was a powerful factor in Paul's involvement in the Judaistic controversy.[83] Hence the readers of Hebrews may well have retained a sense of the continuing validity of the Sinai covenant, and their present need for atonement will encourage them to rely on it as they resume Jewish practices and Jewish fellowship. This is

---

[82] See further the discussion of the use of Exod. 25.40 in Williamson, pp. 560–70.

[83] Jewish religion has been described by E. P. Sanders as 'covenantal nomism': see *Paul and Palestinian Judaism* (London, 1977), especially pp. 421–6.

why it is essential for Hebrews to insist that it has been superseded by the sacrifice of Jesus. To that end he must now show how the death of Jesus has the effect of an atoning sacrifice and at the same time inaugurates the new covenant in which its effect will be permanently available.

THE SACRIFICE OF JESUS

In the light of what Hebrews has said about the new covenant it might be supposed that his argument would be complete if he simply insisted that the old covenant, with all its priestly and sacrificial institutions, had been rendered obselete by the inauguration of the new covenant through the death of Jesus. But this leaves open the question whether the sacrifice of the new covenant can be regarded as a sacrifice for sins. In order to make it absolutely clear that this is so, Hebrews bases his argument on the annual ceremony of the Day of Atonement as it is described in Leviticus 16. This will prove that everything that is essential for atonement has been done in the sacrifice of Christ. Hebrews will then switch to the model of the covenant sacrifice (Exodus 24) to show how this act of atonement has enduring effect, which provides a constant resource to deal with the consciousness of sin, which so deeply troubles his readers.

The choice of the Day of Atonement, which is not explicitly used in connection with the sacrificial death of Jesus elsewhere in the New Testament, is an astute move. As the chief act of atonement in the year, it can be regarded as the primary example of what an act of atonement should be. It thus provides the standard which must be met if the death of Jesus is to be accepted as an atoning sacrifice. As already pointed out, Hebrews argues on the basis of the legal regulations in Leviticus rather than on current practice, because these form the theoretical basis of what is done in the temple.

The Day of Atonement is also a clever choice from the point of view of the actual position of the readers. The whole point of the Day of Atonement is that it removes the burden of all sins throughout the preceding year for which individual atonement has not been made, so long as repentance is sincere. So we read in the Mishnah:

Repentance effects atonement for lesser transgressions against both positive and negative commands in the Law; while for graver transgressions it suspends punishment until the Day of Atonement comes and effects atonement ... For transgressions that are between man and God the Day of Atonement effects atonement, but for transgressions that are between a man and his fellow the Day of Atonement effects atonement only if he has appeased his fellow (m *Yoma* 8.8–9).[84]

Every Jew, however far away from the temple, could feel part of the act, because rest from work, fasting and special prayers were enjoined on everyone. It gave a sense of solidarity with the temple ceremonial, in which reconciliation with God was effected, and also of fellowship with Jews everywhere, because of the high level of local observance. After the fall of Jerusalem the acts of fasting and prayer were felt to be a substitute for the sacrifices, and this idea may well have arisen much earlier in the Diaspora. The Day of Atonement has remained a major annual observance of Jews throughout subsequent centuries.

Thus Hebrews has fastened on the most meaningful aspect of Jewish methods of dealing with the consciousness of sin, which is certain to have exercised a powerful attraction to his readers. It not only has a practical side to it, which is what they need so badly, but also makes up for any lack which they have felt in trying to cope with sin during the preceding year. Modern readers are liable to underestimate the psychological importance of what is involved here. The mental pain of a sense of guilt is too great to be dealt with internally, and needs to be objectified in practical action and to be shared with others who can help to bear the burden. Hebrews knows this well, and this is why he has repeatedly emphasised the humanity and compassion of Jesus as high priest. Now the comparison of the death of Jesus to the sacrifice of the Day of

---

[84] Quoted from H. Danby, *The Mishnah* (Oxford, 1933), p. 172. Note the distinction between sins against other people, for which restitution is possible, and sins against God, for which this is impossible. Obviously the latter are liable to leave an unresolved sense of guilt, unless something equally practical is available.

Atonement can suggest that Christian life under the terms of the new covenant provides for this practical need.

An atonement sacrifice

Just as in the case of Melchizedek in chapter 7, Hebrews begins this section of his argument with some general considerations of the arrangements for the Day of Atonement before coming to the specific application to the death of Jesus. These are given in 9.1–10. First he describes the plan of the tent, which consists of two chambers, the holy place and the holy of holies beyond it, separated by a curtain. He then mentions the contents of the holy of holies, as listed in various references (Exod. 30.1–5; 16.32–3; Num. 17.8–10). We know from Josephus that in New Testament times the holy of holies was completely empty, as the contents were lost at the time of the Babylonian exile and never restored.[85] Hebrews mentions these things so as to make a suitably impressive picture as background to what he really has to say, and excuses himself from going into further detail (verse 5). He makes a mistake in saying that the altar of incense was within the holy of holies, but it does not affect his argument.[86]

The description dwells on two points. As before, these are features which prove that the earthly arrangements are only temporary and are destined to be superseded in the eschatological fulfilment. The first point is the two-chamber pattern of the tent and the second is the extreme restriction on entry into the holy of holies. The holy of holies by its very name indicates

---

[85] There is evidence from Jer. 3.16 that the ark was not restored, but it has been conjectured that the mercy seat (a gold plate with a worshipping cherub facing inwards at each end) was made as a substitute for the ark to indicate the divine presence, just as the ark had represented God's throne. It is only mentioned in the Priestly legislation, where it is treated as a cover on the ark (Exod. 25.17–22; 37.6–9), but 'the room for the mercy seat' in 1 Chr. 28.11 suggests that it was the only object in the holy of holies in the time of the Chronicler (cf. R. de Vaux, *Ancient Israel* (London, 1961), p. 300). However, it must have been lost before the New Testament period in the light of Josephus' description (*War* v.219).

[86] The phrase could be translated 'the golden censer', but this would be even less likely to be kept permanently in the holy of holies, and the meaning 'golden altar of incense' is well attested (see BAG, s.v. *thumiatērion*). The mistake is corrected by transposing the phrase to verse 2 in B and some Sahidic manuscripts.

that it is the place of the presence of God, in so far as his presence can be considered to be localised at all. In the temple of Solomon it seems that the ark within the *debir* (i.e. the holy of holies) was regarded as the pedestal or throne of God unseen above it. Deuteronomy thinks of it as the place of God's name, i.e. the place where his presence is known, thus trying to preserve a more transcendent idea of God. The priestly legislation takes this a stage further by preventing even the priests from entering the holy of holies, so that the entire ceremonial of normal worship is conducted outside in the holy place. The only exception is the entry of the high priest once a year on the Day of Atonement to fill the air above the mercy seat (the cover of the ark, or more probably a substitute for it in the second temple period) with incense and to sprinkle it with sacrificial blood as part of the atoning rites.

From these two facts Hebrews draws the conclusion that direct access to God is not available under the old Law. The elaborate ceremonies of atonement do not in fact establish the relationship with God which belongs to the Messianic age. The annual entry of the high priest into the holy of holies never gets beyond an atoning rite which ought to result in removing the barrier created by sin, but fails to do so. Hebrews sees the two chambers as symbolical, and attributes this to the Holy Spirit (verses 8–9). The Holy Spirit is the author of Scripture considered as prophecy, as we have seen above. So when the description of the tent in Exodus is viewed as a prophetic text it can be applied to the two-stage plan of salvation. The holy place represents the existing temple in which the priestly functions are performed and the holy of holies represents the way into the heavenly sanctuary which belongs to the era of salvation. We may note in passing that these verses support the idea that the temple was still operative when Hebrews was writing.[87]

---

[87] The symbolism has an actual basis in the concept of the holy of holies as the place of the presence of God. It is 'symbolic for the present age' in the sense that the arrangements for the tent are taken in a timeless way to describe the conditions under the old covenant, but the point is made explicit here, because the barrier to entry into the holy of holies is a rare case of a feature of these conditions which

This observation opens the way to a statement of cardinal importance for Hebrews' purpose in verses 9b–10. He points out that the ceremonial which he has just referred to 'cannot perfect the conscience of the worshipper', but can only deal with bodily matters of purification and such-like. He speaks broadly so as to cover the ceremonial laws generally. It is here that he speaks of the consciousness of sin for the first time, which according to my interpretation is the crucial issue. The Greek word *suneidēsis*, used here and in 9.14; 10.2, 22; 13.18, does not quite correspond with the English use of 'conscience'.[88] It does not denote a moral law within the mind, telling one what one ought or ought not to do. It is rather knowledge within oneself of the moral status of one's own actions, whether good or bad, usually the latter. At the end of his letter Hebrews can indicate the integrity with which he has undertaken it by saying that he has a 'clear [literally, good] conscience' (13.18). The problem of the readers is that they are smitten with a consciousness of sin for which they can find no relief without some practical method of atonement with God, and this does not seem to be provided by their Christian allegiance. What Hebrews now says is that the sacrifices and other cleansing rites of the old covenant are a false alternative, because they have only limited value and in any case are only a temporary expedient.

Nearly all modern readers jump to the conclusion that the contrast here is between outward and inward religion. Ceremonial acts cannot ease the consciousness of sin, because that depends on interior repentance and resolve to amend one's life. But if this is what Hebrews means, he simply joins in the well-known protests of the Old Testament prophets about heedless ritualism (one of which he quotes in 10.5–7), and has nothing new to say. However, I think his readers should not be classed with mere ritualists in this way. Psychologically the prescribed ceremonial can play a very important part in

---

actually suggests the intrinsic inadequacy of the old law. The point would have been even more telling if it could have been said that the temple no longer existed.
[88] See C. Maurer, *TDNT*, VII, pp. 898–919; C. A. Pierce, *Conscience in the New Testament* (London, 1955).

helping people to objectify and so to deal with sorrow for sin, just as mourning rites can help people to come to terms with bereavement. Hebrews does not for one moment suggest that the readers are trying to remove their sense of sin by a magic formula.

It is, of course, true that the way in which such ancient rites and ceremonies achieve their stated object was not obvious to people in New Testament times, and indeed the value of animal sacrifices was widely questioned by both Jews and Gentiles in the educated classes to which Hebrews and his readers belong.[89] When he refers in 9.13 to the ashes of a heifer, he touches on an item which is so weird and so apparently unnecessary to his argument that one can scarcely avoid the impression that it is cited purposely to show up the uselessness of these things.[90] In its origins sacrifice did not need explanation, because it was a spontaneous expression of felt needs, and the outward act and the inward meaning were completely at one.[91] But with the emphasis of the post-exilic Jewish community on the codified Law as the revealed will of God, the prescribed ceremonies came to be done not so much for their intrinsic meaning as for the value of obedience in relation to the intention with which they were performed. They were done because they were ordered to be done, and in doing them their inward purpose was achieved. Thus ritual acts need not be unethical, and the prophetic protest is a call to right dispositions in doing them rather than for their abolition.

[89] See J. W. Thompson, 'Hebrews 9 and the Hellenistic Concepts of Sacrifice', *JBL*, 98 (1979), pp. 569ff.

[90] According to Num. 19.9 the heifer was burnt as a sin offering, and the ashes were preserved and used as occasion demanded by sprinkling some of them on water used for cleansing. Apparently the fact that they were derived from a red-coloured animal made them a suitable substitute for blood. Though not mentioned in connection with the Day of Atonement in the OT, Maimonides (*Mishneh Torah* viii.viii.1.4) says that the high priest was twice cleansed in this way during the week before the Day of Atonement. If this is an authentic detail, it could have been known to Hebrews, and so would again support the dating of the letter before the destruction of the temple.

[91] The origins of sacrifice are obscure, and different purposes of it have been suggested in relation to different ancient cultures, but the biblical evidence suggests that the leading idea in ancient Israel was a gift to God to secure his favour. The need for expiation of sin was felt increasingly strongly as time went on, hence the importance

In a sophisticated society, in which there is greater awareness of states of mind, there is often a desire to dispense with outward religious forms, which may be regarded as a hindrance to the reality of religion. Then the motive of obedience is likely to become the only real factor in holding people to the old ways, but it may be assisted by reinterpretation of the ceremonies along acceptable lines. The Alexandrian Jews, and Philo in particular, significantly allegorised them in terms of spiritual states, attaching the details to virtues and vices in the soul, which must be encouraged or avoided.[92] There is no trace of this in Hebrews.

If, then, it is a mistake to class Hebrews as an anti-ritualist, we must look for a different explanation of the contrast which he makes. There is in fact a third factor to be taken into account, and that is the central requirement that the reconciliation, once achieved, should be permanent. This is kept constantly in view by the use of the vocabulary of perfection whenever it is appropriate. We have to remember that perfection in Hebrews is primarily a matter of the completion of God's plan of salvation. Thus the sacrifices prescribed by the Law 'cannot perfect the conscience of the worshipper' (verse 9). On the other hand Christ has entered the heavenly sanctuary 'through [i.e. by means of] the greater and more perfect tent' (verse 11). This is specifically said to be 'not made with hands, that is, not of this creation'. It is clear from verse 14 that the reference is to Christ's offering of himself. This is the means of reconciliation with God, which is foreshadowed in the entry of the high priest into the holy of holies to make atonement each year. The point is summed up in 10.1, where it is said that 'the law has but a shadow of the good things to come' and by its sacrifices 'can never ... make perfect those

of the sin offering in the Priestly legislation. See H.-J. Kraus, *Worship in Israel* (Oxford, 1966), pp. 112–24.

[92] The classic example is *Letter of Aristeas* 128–71. For Philo one may mention the reasons that he gives for the square shape of the altar (Exod. 27.1). The sides are equal 'because all the sacrificial victims which are offered by the heart of a pious mind ought to be equal, whether one offers a hundred bulls or brings (merely) roasted wheat', and the square shape is 'a symbol of the fact that he who offers a sacrifice should stand firm in all respects' (*Questions and Answers on Exodus* II.99 (Loeb translation); cf. *Life of Moses* II.106).

who draw near'. The mere fact that the sacrifices are repeated shows that they do not have permanent effect (10.2).

Thus besides the contrast between inward and outward (or spiritual and material) there is the contrast between the limitations of the old covenant and the lasting condition of the new. For Hebrews the first and last conditions of these two pairs are the same, that is, a truly inward and spiritual cleansing is the same thing as the permanent effect of the new covenant. So the outward ceremonies of the Law are only 'regulations for the body' (verse 10) and avail only for 'the purification of the flesh' (verse 13). Only the sacrifice of the new covenant removes the consciousness of sin permanently. How this happens will be explained in chapter 10.

Nevertheless atonement has certain requirements, and these must be seen to be fulfilled in Jesus. It would be pointless to make such an elaborate proof of his priesthood, unless it was necesssary for him to perform a priestly task. As the received tradition includes the idea of his death as a sacrifice for sins, it is only necessary to show that it fulfilled the conditions suggested by the ceremonial of the Day of Atonement. But when we turn to the text for details, we find that they are surprisingly meagre. We have had one essential point, that it is the one occasion in the year when the high priest enters the holy of holies, and that is specifically for an atonement ritual. Jesus has done this by passing through death to the heavenly sanctuary (verse 12). The account is rather confusing, because Hebrews says that 'he entered once for all into the Holy Place (*ta hagia*)', whereas he ought to have said 'the holy of holies (*ta hagia tōn hagiōn*)'. This, if it is not simply due to textual corruption,[93] can be explained from the fact that Hebrews thinks of heaven as a single-chamber temple, like Revelation 4–5, and indeed 'the sanctuary' in verse 8 is the same Greek expression (*ta hagia*). Logically the first chamber is earth, where the crucifixion took place, but Hebrews does not press the analogy as far as this.[94]

[93] *Ta hagia tōn hagiōn* is read here by one MS (P).
[94] It is, however, implied by the idea that Jesus passed through 'the veil of his flesh' (10.20), for his death in human flesh breaks down the barrier between earth and

This alerts us to the fact that Hebrews is extremely selective in his use of the Day of Atonement regulations, only using the essential items. The most surprising omission is the goat for Azazel (the scapegoat).[95] According to Leviticus 16 two goats are chosen by lot. The first is used for the sacrifice on behalf of all the people, and it is the blood of this goat which is used ceremonially by the high priest when he enters the holy of holies (having previously done the same thing with the blood of the bull which he has sacrificed on behalf of himself and the priesthood). Then he lays his hands on the head of the live goat and confesses over it 'all the iniquities of the people of Israel, and all their transgressions, and all their sins' (Lev. 16.21). It is then taken right away into the wilderness and abandoned. This seems to be a separate ceremony, incorporated into the priestly ritual at a comparatively late stage, probably in response to popular demand. Parallel customs have been noted in the religions of other ancient near eastern peoples, especially in the Babylonian new year festival. Azazel is probably the name of a demon, and is so understood in New Testament times (cf. 1 *Enoch* 8.1; 10.4). The ceremony is a very colourful way of expressing the removal of the people's sins from them to the place where wickedness belongs. As a separate ceremony, it probably served the purpose of conveying the sense of atonement to the people. But when it was incorporated into the priestly rite, it could symbolise only the removal of sins already atoned for by the blood ritual, and it was linked to this previous act by the formal presentation of the live goat to God before the high priest laid his hands on it.

This really explains why Hebrews does not use this detail. The goat for Azazel is not sacrificed and is not used for the

heaven and opens the way for his entry into the heavenly sanctuary. See further p. 102 and n. 105 below.

95 For what follows see de Vaux, *Ancient Israel*, pp. 507–10. Hebrews avoids identifying Jesus with the sacrificed goat as such, but speaks more generally of 'the blood of goats and calves' (9.12–13), so that Jesus is compared to a victim or victims. This helps to smooth the transition to the covenant sacrifice in 9.15–22, where again Hebrews speaks of 'the blood of calves and goats' (verse 19), whereas Exod. 24.5 mentions only oxen (but 'and goats' is omitted by P[46] and a number of other MSS, and could be an addition from the influence of verses 12–13). The scapegoat is first applied to Jesus in *Barn.* 7.6–11.

atonement ritual at all, and – most important from Hebrews' point of view – is not brought into the holy of holies. The idea of Jesus as the scapegoat is not used anywhere in the New Testament. Of course Jesus is represented as bearing the sins of all people, but where this occurs it depends on the application to Jesus of the Suffering Servant prophecy (Isa. 53.4–7, 12; cf. Matt. 8.17; 1 Pet. 2.24–5). There is a clear reference to Isa. 53.12 in the present context in 9.28.

On the other hand Hebrews makes good use of two other features of the Day of Atonement, both obvious, but both essential. The first is that the goat for Yahweh is a proper sacrifice and has to be slain. So we reach the idea that Jesus is not only the true high priest, but is himself the true sacrificial victim. The importance of this for the argument is that it enables Hebrews to claim that, as sacrificial victim, Jesus was 'securing an eternal redemption' (9.12). His priestly offering of sacrifice is done 'once for all' because it is his own death, in which he 'offered himself without blemish to God' (verse 14). It now becomes apparent that the sinlessness of Jesus, which has been mentioned several times previously in other connections, has also qualified him for the role of sacrificial victim. This is a traditional idea, echoed in 1 Pet. 2.19, which refers to 'the precious blood of Christ, like that of a lamb without blemish or spot'.

This brings us to the second point, that the death of the victim releases the blood for the purpose of ceremonial cleansing. The sacrifice is holy, because it has been made over into the sphere of God's holiness, and the blood, which is special and belongs exclusively to God, is available to convey holiness, and therefore cleansing, to people and objects with which it is brought into contact. Though rational, strong-minded people (like Paul with regard to food offered to idols in Romans 14) may assert that there is nothing in it, for many people the sense of objective holiness (which some may prefer to call superstition) remained strong. When Hebrews says that the sprinkling of sacrificial blood 'sanctifies for the purification of the flesh' (verse 13), he does not ridicule such practices, but accepts (at least for the sake of his argument with the readers) that they are good as far as they go, though they cannot deal with sin at the level of inner consciousness and put that right permanently. It is indeed important for him to take the blood-ritual seriously, because according to the theory of atonement implied by the Law it is this which actually effects atonement, which is the central issue for his readers. The point then is that, whether or not the blood-ritual has any value in itself, it is what is prescribed in the Law for atonement and thus has divine sanction for the period of operation of the old covenant and provides the standard to which the death of Jesus must conform, if it is to be accepted as an atonement sacrifice.[96] In fact the analogy cannot be sustained in detail, and this explains the vagueness of Hebrews' expressions in verses 11 and 12, where the preposition *dia* (= through or by means of) is used three times to avoid greater precision of language. Thus 'through the greater and more perfect tent', i.e. by means of a heavenly as opposed to an earthly sphere of operation, Christ entered the heavenly sanctuary, not 'through [RSVm] the blood of goats and calves', i.e. not by means of the blood-ritual of the Day of Atonement, but 'through his own blood', i.e. by means of his own death. So there is no real suggestion of a heavenly blood-ritual, and when Hebrews says in verse 14, 'how much more shall the blood of Christ, who through (*dia*) the eternal Spirit offered himself without blemish to God, purify your conscience ... ', he simply means Christ's death.[97]

The sacrifice of the new covenant

The death of Jesus had the essential features of an atonement sacrifice. But that does not in itself prove either that it was unrepeatable or that it could remove the consciousness of sin

---

[96] It might be supposed from the final words of 9.22 that it is the shedding of blood, i.e. the slaughter of the victim, which effects forgiveness. But it has been shown by T. C. G. Thornton ('The Meaning of *haimatekchusia* in Heb. ix.22', *JTS*, 15 (1964), 63–5) that what is meant is the sprinkling of blood, as is clear in the present context. The death of the victim is only preparatory, to release the blood for its ceremonial purpose.

[97] For 'through the eternal Spirit' see pp. 57–8 above.

permanently. So now Hebrews resumes the theme of the new covenant which he has introduced at length in chapter 8. He had already prepared for this shift of focus in 9.11 when he said that 'Christ appeared as a high priest of the good things that have come'.[98] For this means that the blessings of the coming age or era of the new covenant have already become available through his priestly act. So in verse 15 Jesus is described as 'the mediator of a new covenant'. He died a sacrificial death 'so that those who are called may receive the promised eternal inheritance'. In order to show that what has been achieved really is permanent in its effect, Hebrews must make the point that it has an essentially permanent character. This is why he takes up the idea of the covenant, because, whereas an atonement sacrifice deals with past sins, a covenant sacrifice inaugurates a permanent arrangement for the future. Once a covenant has been solemnly inaugurated with the sanctions of a sacrifice it can be expected to remain in force. That is what is argued in 9.15–28.

At this point Hebrews makes a move which is often thought to be an unwarrantable sleight of hand. He takes advantage of the range of meaning of the Greek word for covenant (*diathēkē*), which can also be used to denote a last will and testament. He points out that a will does not come into force until the testator has died. Therefore, he argues, a death is necessary for a covenant to come into force. This happened in the case of the Sinai covenant, because a covenant sacrifice is described in Exod. 24.4–8. It was necessary for the inauguration of the new covenant too. Some scholars, notably Westcott and Nairne, have tried to remove the slur on Hebrews' integrity by arguing that the meaning 'testament' is not intended here, but 'covenant' is maintained through the relevant passage (verses 16–17). But this can be done only by a very strained exegesis. In fact Hebrews is not juggling with words so as take advantage of double meanings to slip in an invalid argument. From his point of view 'testament' is part of the meaning of *diathēkē*,

---

98 The reading 'that have come' (P[46] B D* 1739 d sy [(p).h]) is accepted as original by most modern scholars against the majority of later MSS, which read 'the good things to come', probably influenced by 10.1.

and it suggests to him a useful *comparison*. It is no more than that. Just as the death of a person brings that person's testament into effect, so the ratification of a covenant by means of a sacrifice brings the covenant into force. To put it another way, a *diathēkē*, which means both covenant and testament, normally requires a death to bring it into effect.

Next Hebrews notes that, just as in the atonement sacrifice, and indeed in the regulations of the Law in general (verses 21–2), the covenant sacrifice includes a blood-ritual to cleanse and sanctify the people and the book, or instrument, of the covenant. He actually quotes Exod. 24.8, in which Moses refers to 'the blood of the covenant'. As far as the application to Jesus is concerned, this again simply means his death. But Nairne is surely right in seeing here an allusion to the eucharistic words of Jesus at the Last Supper (Mark 14.24). However, there may be a further connection, because the Last Supper tradition may have suggested the 'testament' concept, if the institution narrative, with the *anamnēsis* command ('do this ... in remembrance of me', 1 Cor. 11.25), is regarded as Jesus' testament to his followers as he prepares for his death. We should not exclude the possibility that Hebrews presupposes that what he has to say about the continuing validity of the covenant will chime in with the readers' experience of fellowship with Jesus in the celebration of the eucharist.[99]

Hebrews rounds off the argument up to this point in verses 23–8 with a very useful summary of what has been proved so far. The status of all these sacrificial institutions as 'copies of the heavenly things' is recalled to show their inadequacy and impermanence. Again we must remember that the issue is not the anti-ritualist contrast of inward and outward religion as such, but the scope of cleansing of the conscience. Hebrews next makes the point that Christ's sacrifice is intrinsically unrepeatable. This is proved by the fact that there is no previous history of his death over and over again. On the

---

[99] The eucharistic accounts of Mark 14.22–5 and parallels and 1 Cor. 11.23–6 have probably survived from their use as the 'charter story' for the church's celebration of the eucharist, and so would be known independently to Hebrews and his readers: see G. D. Kilpatrick. *The Eucharist in Bible and Liturgy* (Cambridge, 1983), pp. 69–80.

contrary his death is the eschatological atonement sacrifice, which has happened 'once for all at the end of the age'. Then he introduces a new point, that it is the commonly held conviction that judgment follows death. So the death of Jesus too must be followed by judgment, and this indeed will happen at the parousia, when he 'will appear a second time' for this purpose. However, it will be 'not to deal with sin',[100] for that has been done already, 'but to save those who are eagerly waiting for him'.

Here we must pause to observe that this is the one point where Hebrews indicates his understanding of the state of the dead. To the modern reader it looks as if he thinks that the death of each person is followed immediately by an individual judgment. This then appears to conflict with the idea of the second coming of Christ, which seems to have no purpose. However, what Hebrews says is consistent with what is said in other books of the New Testament, and reflects views commonly held by Jews at this time.[101] At death the body is placed in the grave, but the soul goes to a place of waiting until the final judgment. Then the bodies rise from the graves and are reunited with the souls at the general resurrection, judgment is given, and those who are saved have their part in the eternal kingdom. This is exactly what is implied in Paul's teaching in 1 Thess. 4.13–17. In his longer explanation in 1 Corinthians 15 he argues that the reconstituted body is a transformed body, a spiritual and incorruptible body suited to the eternal kingdom. But there is a preliminary judgment at death inasmuch as there are different places of waiting for the souls of different classes of persons, some nearer to God than others. This idea also is reflected in Paul, who expects to be 'with Christ' during the period of waiting, so that he longs to die for this reason (Phil. 1.23). Similarly in Rev. 6.9–11 the souls of the martyrs are seen to be waiting under the heavenly altar, which is the nearest possible place to God himself.

---

100 Literally 'without sin', but the context shows that this means, not 'as one who is sinless' as in 4.15, but without again having to bear the sins of many (see Spicq *ad loc.*).

101 Cf. G. W. E. Nicklesburg, *Resurrection, Immortality, and Eternal Life in Intertestamental Judaism* (Cambridge, MA, 1972).

It is obvious on this understanding of the state of the departed that those like Paul who are 'with Christ' have nothing to fear at the judgment. Hebrews shares this view. Those who are with Christ already enjoy the benefit of his atoning sacrifice, and there is no need of a fresh act of atonement 'to deal with sin' at the parousia, or second coming, which marks the completion of God's plan of salvation for all people.

The will of God for sanctification

Because the act of atonement has been completed by the death of Christ, it can be confidently affirmed that God's plan of salvation has now come into operation. In other words, the era of the new covenant, which properly belongs to the time after the parousia, is already in force for those who have been brought within its scope by their conversion to Christianity. This has practical consequences. A covenant is an agreement between two parties. Each side is under obligation to act according to the agreed stipulations. So Hebrews brings his exposition of the sacrificial death of Jesus to a conclusion in 10.1–18 by showing how God's will is by the new covenant unalterably directed towards the sanctification and perfection (completion) of those who approach him through Christ. This is God's side in the covenant. The people's side, which we shall consider in the next section, is the response of faith, which for Hebrews is not merely a state of mind, but has definite practical expression in the life of the church.

Continuing the summary of the argument just given in 9.23–8, Hebrews reminds the readers of the temporary status of the Law and the inability of the sacrifices under it to produce a permanent effect (10.1–2). The mere fact that the Day of Atonement takes place every year proves that the sense of need for forgiveness of sins remains, and this is because 'it is impossible that the blood of bulls and goats should take away sins' (verse 4). This of course refers to the removal of sins permanently, but it also suggests an inherent impossibility, that there is something about the very nature of animal sacrifice and the blood-ritual which prevents it from achieving the object of taking away sins. It may well be that a common opinion was that the value of these ceremonies simply resided in the moral obedience involved in carrying out what the Law required, as suggested above. Whatever people thought about this, the mere assumption, implicit in the Law itself, that the blood-ritual is intended to remove sin raises the question how it was supposed to do so, and this in its turn raises the question with regard to the sacrifice of Jesus. In the case of Jesus the theory of the moral value of obedience provides precisely the answer which Hebrews needs. Hebrews now seizes this to place the coping-stone on his argument.

So in 10.5–10 he takes up a suitable text from Ps. 40.6–8, in which the psalmist asserts that God does not want sacrifices but obedience to his will, and solemnly vows that that is what he will do. The passage is typical of the prophetic passages on sacrifice and obedience, in which the contrast formula 'this *and not* that' is an idiomatic way of saying 'this *more than* that' (cf. Hosea 6.6). However, Hebrews takes the contrast literally, and sees the passage as a prophecy of the new order in which sacrifices will be abolished (verse 9). But the passage also serves his purpose in other ways. Because he understands it prophetically he is able to identify the speaker with Christ himself, so that what is said applies to him specifically. Moreover, the Septuagint text reads 'a body you have prepared for me', which differs from the original Hebrew ('you have given me an open ear'). Hebrews shows no knowledge of this difference. He simply accepts the Septuagint text, which splendidly suits his purpose, because it suggests the purpose of the incarnation. When the Wisdom/Word/Son of God came to fullest expression in the human Jesus it was expressly to do God's will by completing the plan of salvation. So the words of the psalm are the utterance of God's Son 'when he came into the world' (verse 5).[102] Thereby he fulfils what 'is

---

[102] Cf. the very similar phrase in 1.6 and the comments on it on p. 34 above. The RSV text reads, 'When Christ came into the world', but 'Christ' is not in the Greek text, and if it is necessary to insert the subject it would be better to say 'the Son'.

written in the roll of the book' (verse 7), i.e. his destiny.[103] His will to do the will of God obviously applies also to his sacrifice of himself on the cross. So it is 'by that will', conformed to God's will, that 'we have been sanctified through the offering of the body of Jesus Christ once for all' (verse 10). The language of this verse significantly reflects 2.11–15, where Hebrews uses the expression 'sanctified' and stresses the fact that Jesus shared our 'flesh and blood' in his death. This shows the consistency of his presentation and the control which he exercises over the argument from start to finish.

The sacrifice of Christ, being in accordance with God's will, results in the invitation to sit at God's right hand. These words of the foundation text Ps. 110.1 are recalled in 10.12–13, including the continuation 'till I make your enemies your footstool'. This indicates a time of waiting until the process of the conquest of sin is complete. There is a close parallel to this idea in 1 Cor. 15.25, where these words are similarly applied to the time between the ascension and the parousia. Here, then, Hebrews is in line with the classic formulation of eschatology in early Christianity.

Finally the notion of the will of God brings the thought back to the conditions of the new covenant. Making a literary inclusion with chapter 8, Hebrews quotes again in verses 16 and 17 the last two verses of the new covenant prophecy, Jer. 31.33 and 34. The first of these asserts that under the new covenant God will put his 'laws on their hearts and write them on their minds'. This means that the people will be enabled to do God's will. It is their side of the covenant, which we shall consider further in the next section. God's side is then stated in the other verse: 'I will remember their sins and their misdeeds no more.' That is God's intention in bringing the new covenant into effect, and so it represents his unalterable will for our sanctification. So Hebrews comments, 'Where there is forgiveness of these, there is no longer any offering for sin' (verse 18).

---

[103] The idea of a heavenly book, containing the names of the living, was widespread in the ancient near east: see Exod. 32.32–3; Ps. 87.6; Luke 10.20; Rev. 20.12, 15. For a book of destiny, see Ezek. 3.1–3; Rev. 5.1. The idea has been the subject of a special study by L. Koep, *Das himmlische Buch in Antike und Christentum* (Bonn, 1952).

Thus through the sacrifice of Christ the conditions have been established in which the problem of the readers is solved. Though they cannot avoid sin altogether during the period of waiting before the parousia, their participation in the new covenant ensures that they have the means of coping with it. They need not be held back by any fear of divine wrath, because the will of God for their salvation is secure. All they need to do is to apply the behaviour which belongs to their own side in the covenant, which can be summed up as the response of faith.

THE RESPONSE OF FAITH

Hebrews has finished his exposition of the sacrifice of Christ. It has occupied a large segment of his letter, stretching from 7.1 to 10.18. It has also required close attention on the part of the readers, as it is quite complex and uses ideas which have not previously been employed in the basic Christian teaching. But this does not mean that the argument is finished. There is still the practical side to be explained. This takes the form of renewed moral exhortation, balancing the exhortations which preceded the main argument in chapter 6. But it is a mistake to think of this as a general exhortation to the life of faith in response to the inspiring exposition which has just been given. On the contrary, it leads into the practical conclusion which is the whole purpose of the argument, and to which all that precedes can be regarded as merely preparatory. The readers are asked to accept the main argument, because it provides the grounds for understanding what they ought to do in order to cope with their consciousness of sin.

It has been suggested above that this is the people's side of the covenant, but Hebrews does not actually say so. Nevertheless what he has to say does amount to an exposition of God's promise that 'I will put my laws on their hearts, and write them on their minds' (10.16). So in the remainder of chapter 10 he takes up the thought of 'receiving knowledge of the truth' (verse 26) and shows how the proper response to it is the quality of faith. This will then be reinforced by the deliberately long and inspiring catalogue of examples of faith in chapter 11 before the whole argument is brought to its conclusion in chapter 12.

Practical application

The practical application takes the form of an exhortation because it is what Hebrews wants the readers to do. First he summarises the argument on atonement once more in 10.19–21. This is to make it clear that the practical application arises directly out of the argument. It will assist our understanding of the theology of Hebrews to observe those points which he singles out for mention. First 'we have confidence to enter the sanctuary', and that means the heavenly presence of God. There is no longer any barrier of sin preventing access to God. Secondly this has been achieved 'by the blood of Jesus'. This is a traditional formula (cf. Rom. 3.25; 5.9; Eph. 2.13; 1 Pet. 1.19; Rev. 1.5; 5.9; 7.14), which has no doubt been used in the original teaching given to the readers on their conversion. Thirdly the death of Jesus is the dedication of a 'new and living way' into the sanctuary. Hebrews uses here an unusual word for 'new' (*prosphatos*) to convey the nuance that it was not previously available.[104] It is a 'living' way in the sense that it gives life. Both words suggest that this way to the presence of God is appropriate to the new age and the new covenant. Fourthly, just as access to the holy of holies was through the curtain separating it from the holy place, so the entry of Jesus had the character of passing from the earthly sphere to the heavenly, and this was by means of his death in mortal flesh. The strange identification of the curtain with the flesh of Jesus has caused needless complications of exegesis,[105] but it is clear

---

104   It generally means 'fresh' or 'recent', and is the word used in the LXX of Eccles. 1.9, 'There is nothing new under the sun.'

105   Three main factors affect the exegesis of this passage. (a) There is the question whether Hebrews knows and alludes to the portent of the tearing of the veil at the time of the death of Jesus, reported in Mark 15.38. This has led to the conclusion that Hebrews identifies the flesh of Jesus with the veil precisely because his flesh was 'torn' in the crucifixion. But Hebrews does not make this point and shows no knowledge of the Markan tradition. The reference is not to the tearing of the veil, but to the ceremonial of the Day of Atonement, in which the high priest passes

from the total thrust of the argument of Hebrews that it is intended to give just a hint of one of his fundamental positions, which is the solidarity of Jesus with humanity (2.14; 5.7). Finally the sense of solidarity implied in 'flesh' is enhanced by the statement that 'we have a great high priest over the house of God', which reminds us that the priesthood of Jesus is as much a metaphor as it is a theological truth (2.17) and the church has been referred to as God's house (3.1–6). Taking these five points in reverse order, we can make a brief summary of the whole argument: Jesus, as our own representative, died in human flesh, which inaugurated the new covenant because it was a sacrifice for sins, and thereby gives us confidence to enter the presence of God himself. From this point of view he is our pioneer (2.10; 12.2).

On this basis Hebrews invites the readers to 'draw near' (verse 22). They should do so 'with a true heart in full assurance of faith'. This is in fact their side in the new covenant, as has just been indicated in the quotation from Jeremiah in verse 16. The crucial quality is faith, and the meaning of it will be clarified later. But faith takes as its starting point the completed work of Christ, and the most important aspect of this from the point of view of the situation of the readers is that it has secured forgiveness of sins. So at last it can be said that we have 'our hearts sprinkled clean from an evil conscience', that is, from the misery of the consciousness of sin. So, to speak metaphorically, we have 'our bodies washed with pure water'. There may be an allusion here to baptism,

---

beyond the veil into the holy of holies (9.3). (b) From this point of view the veil is a barrier which must be removed before he gains access to God. But in fact his sacrifice was carried out in the flesh. For this reason Westcott, followed by Montefiore, takes the words 'that is, through his flesh' (RSV) to qualify 'the new and living way' (cf. NEB 'the way of his flesh'). But the Greek order of words is against this, and there is no need to take such a negative view of the veil, as it is the means of entry into the divine presence just as much as it is the barrier to the vision of God. In 5.7 'the days of his flesh' means his human life, and so here the humanity of Jesus is the condition in which he died (his 'blood', verse 19), thus opening the way into the sanctuary. (c) Wilson gives details of later Gnostic statements which use the idea of the veil to suggest the necessity of passing beyond the flesh to attain the life of the spirit, but he rightly rejects the suggestion that this is what Hebrews means. The choice of language here is intended to recall the substance of the preceding argument, not to say something new.

but if so it is only to recall the memory of that as a past event which should have created a continuing sense of being cleansed from sin. But the words certainly allude to Ezek. 36.25, in which the metaphor is used in a passage which has close links with the new covenant prophecy of Jeremiah.

It is important to see that this is an intellectual position, the knowledge and conviction that the state of reconciliation has been achieved permanently. It still falls short of providing a practical programme for the readers. But in their worried state of conscience a convincing intellectual argument is not sufficient. So in verses 23–5 Hebrews outlines four practical things which they ought to do. These are important, because they embody his alternative to the disastrous tendency to resume Jewish purificatory practices, which are threatening to draw the readers away from their Christian allegiance altogether. Not surprisingly, these points are four good reasons for maintaining Christian life. We must now try to see how far they constitute a suitable practical programme.

The first thing is to 'hold fast the confession of our hope without wavering, for he who promised is faithful' (verse 23). At first sight this looks as if it lacks practical expression, but in fact it has a practical side of great value. For what is recommended is a continual effort to remember the confession that Christ has died for our sins in the knowledge that God is faithful to his promise given in the new covenant prophecy. This is the God whom we are liable to offend by our daily sins. So remembering his true attitude can be an insurance against allowing despondency to take hold of our minds, and so drive us to obsolete practices in the vain attempt to put matters right. The grand scale of the preceding argument on the sacrifice of Christ should have gone far to renew in the readers the conviction that God is faithful in this way. So this first point can be seen as an exhortation to the readers to keep their heads, and not to be thrown off balance by undue anxiety.

Secondly Hebrews recommends mutual support in the common endeavour to live the Christian life, which consists of 'love and good works' (verse 24). This is not only because 'almsgiving ... will purge away every sin' (Tobit 12.9), but because the mutual love which is basic to the early Christian ethic takes the form of a shared response to the love of God himself displayed in the sacrifice of Christ and so is done for his sake (cf. 6.10). This point thus looks to the positive value of practical fellowship in maintaining the sense of solidarity with the rest of the redeemed. The readers will not be helped if they feel that they are cut off on account of their sins.

Thirdly this applies specially to the Christian assembly, which some of the readers have begun to neglect, either through discouragement or because of pressure from their Jewish friends. This is a crucial factor, because the assembly is the occasion for the corporate liturgical commemoration of the sacrifice of Christ, which is the theme of the Christian sacrifice of praise (13.15).[106] Participation in the liturgy more than anything else provides the practical programme which the readers need. There is no hint here of disciplinary exclusion. Theirs is a case of self-exclusion, and it is disastrous, because it removes them from the setting in which they have active participation in the gospel of reconciliation between each other and God, sealed (if the assembly takes the form of the eucharist) with the communion of the body and blood of Christ (cf. 1. Cor 10.16).

Fourthly the readers should not forget that the time is short and the Day is drawing near (verse 25). Retaining a strong sense of the imminence of the parousia, Hebrews wants them to persevere expectantly and not to shrink back (verses 38–9) on the grounds that maintaining Christian life is too much of a struggle (verse 32).

Thus, though no specific purification practices are made available, there are instead various aspects of ordinary Christian life which make the fact of Christ's atoning work and the certainty of God's will for our salvation constantly present to the mind, calling forth the response of the heart, and thereby renewing the sense of unbreakable fellowship with God. The wound of the consciousness of sin is healed, because the soul's

---

[106] Cf. the liturgy described in Revelation 4–5, which P. Prigent claims to reflect the actual Christian liturgy, corresponding with the morning service of the synagogue: (i) praise for creation (Rev. 4.9–11); (ii) the bringing of the Torah scroll (Rev. 5.1–5); (iii) praise for redemption (Rev. 5.6–14): P. Prigent, *Apocalypse et liturgie* (Neuchâtel, 1964), pp. 46–76.

access to God is found to be unbroken. Our great high priest knows our weaknesses (4.15) and always lives to make intercession for us (7.25). It is not expected that we shall miraculously live without sin, even if the time of waiting for the parousia is still expected to be short. But provided, of course, that we repent, the remedy is always available simply in persevering in the acts which impress the central message of the gospel on our minds. These things constantly renew faith, and faith is the one essential quality for those who would 'keep their souls' (verse 39).

Warning to keep faith

Before launching into this exposition of faith, Hebrews makes a severe warning of the dire effects of apostasy in 10.26–31, comparable to 6.6–8. This is not just to balance the earlier warning from the point of view of artistic construction, but much more to serve a similar purpose from the point of view of what follows. Just as the length and importance of the exposition of the sacrifice of Jesus required an effort to win the most careful attention of the readers, so also the exposition of faith is crucial to their understanding. This is because it is the proper frame of mind for Christian living, as will be shown. The comparison with the previous passage shows that the exhortation in 10.19–25 which we have just considered functions as an introduction to the exposition of faith, like the passage on the priesthood of Jesus in 5.1–10. Thus in each case there is an introduction to the subject, then a solemn warning, and then the full exposition.

The warning refers to deliberate sin (verse 26). As before, we must beware of applying this to all kinds of grave sins, or to 'mortal' sin as opposed to 'venial' sin. The context makes it clear that the reference is to apostasy, which is the deliberate rejection of that act of God in Christ which has actually secured the forgiveness of sins. Those who do this 'spurn the Son of God', i.e. God's agent for our salvation, 'profane the blood of the covenant by which they have been sanctified', as if the sacrifice of Jesus expounded in chapter 9 meant nothing, and 'outrage the Spirit of grace', by denying their own baptismal endowment.[107]

As before, it is probable that Hebrews is referring to what he fears might happen, rather than what has actually happened. His statement that 'there no longer remains a sacrifice for sins' (verse 26) must be understood in the light of the theology of chapters 7–9: the sacrifices under the old covenant have now been superseded, and the sacrifice of Christ is the one unrepeatable sacrifice of the new covenant, and so leaves open no alternative. It is not implied that, if the readers did apostatise and subsequently repent, they could never again claim the benefit of the sacrifice of Christ.

However, as before, Hebrews softens the harshness of the warning, with its awesome references to the divine judgment (verses 27–31), by another *captatio benevolentiae*, recalling the excellent record of the readers at the time of their conversion (verses 32–4).[108] Then they were willing to endure much hardship, as they had an eye to their heavenly reward. Now they are urged not to throw this away by losing confidence (verses 35–6). According to my interpretation this is precisely the problem. Since the joyful days of the beginning of their conversion the readers have lost confidence in the truth of the gospel, and this is why they are in such a quandary about their consciousness of sin. It is obvious that the main reason for this is the delay of the parousia, for which they were not prepared. Hebrews sees a parallel in the position of the prophet Habakkuk (late seventh century BC), who was expecting a divine act of deliverance imminently, but was tempted to give up hope on account of the failure of the expected help to materialise. So he now quotes Hab. 2.3–4 to assert three things: that the parousia is near, that faith is required during the time of waiting, and that God will reject those who shrink back from keeping faith (verses 37–8). All these points are directly relevant to the

---

[107] On 'the Spirit of grace' see n. 45 above.

[108] If Italy is the destination of the letter, the sufferings referred to may be the expulsion of Jews from Rome by Claudius in AD 49 (see p. 18 above). Otherwise it may be disturbances caused by the uncompromising position of the original missionaries (2.3; 13.7), who required the converts to separate from the synagogue, resulting in hostility on the part of the local pagan population as well.

situation, and the quotation gives a splendid opening for his exposition of faith in the next chapter. It is probable that this quotation, which has to some extent been adapted,[109] had long been used in Christian circles. Part of it, that the righteous will live by faith, was seized on by Paul as a main support for his special argument on justification by faith (Gal. 3.11; Rom. 1.17). One alteration of the text which can be confidently attributed to Hebrews himself is the reversal of the two clauses of Hab. 2.4, which makes 'my righteous one' the subject of both clauses. This can then be directly applied to the readers, who may either shrink back and be destroyed or have faith and keep their souls (verse 39). So the ground is prepared for the exposition of faith in chapter 11.

Faith in Hebrews

The quality of faith has already been indicated by small touches in the preceding exhortations, which show that it is the proper response to the sacrifice of Christ and can be regarded as the human side in the new covenant. Thus the readers 'have confidence' (10.19). They are to 'hold fast the confession of our hope without wavering' (verse 23), but rather to have 'full assurance of faith' (verse 22). Faith can be described as the reception process, without which the gospel of reconciliation through the atoning sacrifice of Christ remains merely theoretical and unassimilated. It is therefore an attitude of mind which is essential to the completion of the process of salvation.

---

[109] Hab. 2.3 has been shortened by replacing most of the verse with an idiomatic phrase (perhaps taken from Isa. 26.20 LXX) which means 'a little while'. Then the LXX's literal rendering of the Hebrew idiom 'coming it [i.e. the vision] will come [i.e. come to pass]', which properly means 'it will surely come to pass', is personalised ('coming he will come' = 'he will surely come'), and this has been taken a stage further in Hebrews, reading it as 'the coming one will come'. In Hab. 2.4 = verse 38 the two halves of the verse are reversed. It is disputed whether the original LXX took 'my' with 'righteous one', as in Hebrews, or with 'faith', but in any case it represents a different reading of the Hebrew text of Habakkuk, which has 'by his faithfulness' and no pronoun with 'righteous one'. The LXX also attests a different reading of the Hebrew at the beginning of the other half ('shrinks back' for 'puffed up') and again has 'my' for 'his'. There is a probable allusion to Hab. 2.3 in 2 Pet. 3.9. The Habakkuk Commentary from Qumran shows another roughly contemporary application of these verses in a sectarian Jewish context.

So it is not just a matter for a pep-talk, in spite of the bracing and vivid style of chapter 11. In fact there is a definite intellectual position with regard to faith in this chapter, which is carefully composed to draw the readers into full understanding of what it means and to inspire them to respond wholeheartedly.

Faith in Hebrews is a moral quality of firmness, fidelity, and reliability as in normal biblical usage.[110] It is an attribute of God, who keeps faith with his people, as we have just seen in 10.23. The same idea is found in Paul (for example 1 Cor. 1.9) and other New Testament writers. Hebrews refers to Moses as a human example of faithfulness in 3.1–6. He there states that Jesus was similarly faithful in his care for God's people. The same quality is required of Christians themselves (3.6, 14). In our consideration of these passages in a previous section it was pointed out that Hebrews does not use 'faith' to denote the content of Christian belief. That is denoted by the word 'confession', used only at 3.1; 4.14; 10.23. Also Hebrews shows no knowledge of the specialised use of 'faith' developed by Paul in connection with the Judaistic controversy, and expounded in Galatians and Romans. Paul's doctrine of justification by faith means the acceptance of God's justifying grace as a gift (Rom. 3.24–5) by contrast with the claim that performance of the works of the Law is required to secure justification in the sight of God. Thus the emphasis in Paul falls on the acceptance of unmerited blessing gained through the gospel of redemption. From this point of view faith for Paul is the starting point for Christian life and so carries with it a strong sense of the content of the confession of faith. Christian life is lived on the basis of faith, and Paul can even say that behaviour that is not based on faith is sin (Rom. 14.23). This is all so different from Hebrews that it is not surprising that Luther was easily convinced that Hebrews could not have been written by Paul.

However, it would be a mistake to press the difference between Hebrews and Paul so far as to suggest that their views are incompatible. It is really a difference of emphasis in

---

[110] Cf. R. Bultmann, '*pisteuō, ktl*', *TDNT*, vi, pp. 174–228; E. Grässer, *Der Glaube im Hebräerbrief* (Marburg, 1965).

response to entirely different circumstances. Paul is arguing that Gentile converts should not be forced to accept circumcision and the obligations of the Jewish Law against a strong lobby which was insisting on this. Hebrews is dealing with Jewish converts in a situation where the Christian community required abandonment of the Law, and their loss of faith is tempting them to return to it. For his argument Paul plays down the element of moral firmness in faith, because that would come dangerously close to affirming the value of independent human effort, which is precisely what is wrong with justification by works of the Law. Hebrews agrees that faith is the proper response to God's act of salvation through Christ, but he sees it as a moral quality which should be constantly expressed in Christian living.

In fact it is possible to be more specific than this. Hebrews gives a definition of faith in 11.1, and then proceeds to illustrate it from numerous examples. The length and impressiveness of the chapter are adjusted to the scale of the whole epistle, so as to make the issue carry its due weight in relation to the total argument of which it is an essential part. The examples would all be familiar to the readers and are calculated to appeal to their imagination. They are derived mostly from the Old Testament, but end with allusions to the Maccabees and the contemporary *Lives of the Prophets*, which were popular among Hellenistic Jews and probably used for moral instruction.[111]

The definition is that 'faith is the assurance of things hoped for, the conviction of things not seen'. This is not a philosophical definition of faith but a thoroughly practical one. The Greek word for 'assurance' (*hupostasis*, translated 'substance' in AV) became a key word in later doctrinal controversy, in which the translation 'substance' is often correct. It has this meaning in Heb. 1.3, where it is translated 'nature' in RSV, referring to the divine nature. In 3.14, however, it was translated 'confidence', and it clearly has this meaning in 2 Cor. 9.4;

---

[111] 4 Maccabees (English text in Charlesworth, *Pseudepigrapha*, II, pp. 531–43) is a Jewish commendation of Stoic virtue, using the example of the martyrs described in 2 Maccabees 6–7. *The Lives of the Prophets* (ibid., pp. 385–99) is a brief collection of anecdotes and curious facts about the prophets.

11.17. Both meanings are common in Greek usage generally, and both are derived meanings from the more literal meaning 'foundation'. In the present context faith is the foundation of a positive attitude towards the future, which cannot yet be experienced but has to remain a matter of hope. It is not the nature of the future, but the basis for a relation to the future.[112] This is clarified by the synonymous expression, 'the conviction of things not seen'. Here the word for 'conviction', *elenchos*, which occurs only here in the New Testament, has the basic meaning of 'testing'. Faith tests the unseen things by acting as though they were present and visible. It is a positive conviction expressed in action. Though 'things not seen' could refer to timeless realities, the parallel suggests that the real reference is to the future. So faith is a frame of mind in which we confidently make trial of what is promised in the future.

The numerous examples all show people acting in this way. Each one starts with the expression 'by faith', a literary device of repetition technically called anaphora, which has a powerful emotional effect. Modern readers are liable to misunderstand what is meant by it. It does not mean 'by means of faith', i.e. using a technique of auto-suggestion or working on the suggestibility of others, in the way of some faith-healers. What it means is 'acting on the basis of faith'.[113] Each person's action is guided by a promise concerning the future at a time when it is impossible to see the outcome, so that they can only act in faith. This even applies to the first item on the list, which is concerned with the act of creation (verse 3). For the common understanding of creation, shared by Hebrews and his readers, always involves an act of faith, inasmuch as it is assumed that the visible created order is the result of a divine *fiat* (Gen. 1.3), whereby things that were unseen, being only ideas in God's mind, were brought into actuality. This is not something that we can see or prove, but it is something that we (i.e. Hebrews and his readers) take for

---

[112] H. Koester, *'hupostasis'*, *TDNT*, VIII, pp. 585ff, has attempted to make out a case for 'nature'. See the discussion in Wilson, p. 202.

[113] Hence *pistei* is dative of manner, not of instrument: see Spicq, II, p. 340.

granted. It is probable that this item is included in the list so as to show the principle at work from the beginning of the biblical record.[114]

Then follows the list of those who acted in faith and 'received divine approval' (verse 2) accordingly. In each case the act of the person concerned preceded the actual realisation of what was hoped for or promised. Even if they gained their immediate ends, this was not the fulfilment of the promise in its deepest sense, for that belongs to the age to come (see verses 13–16). And so at the end of the chapter we read that 'all these, well attested by their faith, did not receive what was promised, since God had foreseen something better for us, that apart from us they should not be made perfect' (verses 39–40). Obviously this cannot refer to perfection of character, but must mean the completion of God's plan. The people of old all contributed to the working out of God's plan in so far as they acted in faith, but they never saw the ultimate goal. This was not reached until Christ came to inaugurate the eschatological era of the new covenant, as the whole of the preceding argument has shown. It is left to the readers to assume that, once the plan is complete, i.e. in the general resurrection which is soon to take place at the parousia, these people's time of waiting in paradise will come to an end and they will receive their due reward.

Jesus the pioneer and perfecter of faith

Having given such an elaborate and stirring portrayal of the meaning of faith, Hebrews is now intent on rounding off the argument in such a way as to leave his readers inspired to follow it out in practice. Jesus is the climax of the examples of faith, because it is he who alone inaugurated the fulfilment of God's eschatological plan of salvation and also carried it through in his own person. He is thus both the pioneer and the perfecter (completer) of the act of faith which is required of the

---

[114] It should be observed that Hebrews is concerned only with the fact that belief in creation requires faith in the sense in which it is used in this chapter, and does not intend to give a doctrine of creation. Thus it is a mistake to assume that he wishes to promote a doctrine of creation *ex nihilo*, or that he disregards the function of God's Son in creation (see 1.1–3).

readers. He shared the same aim as the readers, which is abiding fellowship with God, here called 'the joy that was set before him' (12.2). He provided the example of the way in which this aim could be achieved in that he 'endured the cross, despising the shame'. This was of course his unique act of atonement, but it is also a matter of moral example, and that is the issue at this moment. The result was that he took his place in heaven, 'seated at the right hand of the throne of God'. And so the completion of the process is described in the traditional language of Ps. 110.1.

If faith, i.e. acting in faith, is primarily a matter of following the example of Jesus, then it is clear that the struggle against sin must be maintained (12.1, 4), and the readers must be prepared for suffering. It is significant that Hebrews does not suggest that they ought not to have a sense of sin. He knows well that it 'clings so closely'.[115] But one aspect of the life of faith is the constant endeavour to throw it off with the confidence that comes from knowing that atonement has been secured once and for all. In fact the struggle against sin itself entails suffering. The readers have already been commended for their endurance in the early days of their conversion (10.32–4). But now Hebrews points out that 'you have not yet resisted to the point of shedding your blood' (12.4). It has been suggested that this proves that Hebrews was written before the Neronian persecution of AD 64, but that would only apply if the destination of the letter was Rome, and this is quite uncertain. It is more likely that the thought of the supreme test of martyrdom has been prompted by the model of Jesus himself. It is only a fleeting reference, and Hebrews prefers to concentrate on the conventional analogy of fatherly discipline, which suggests the educative value of suffering. This suffering could be the harassment of Jewish pressure to apostatise, if we are right in thinking that the major problem is the attempt of unbelieving Jews to win them back by playing on their consciences in respect of sin.

Faith also consists in the will to 'run with perseverance the race that is set before us' (verse 1). This suggests a positive

---

[115] On the Greek word, see n. 49 above.

striving after virtue. Some suggestions are made in verses
12–17. We may notice particularly the exhortation to 'strive for
peace with all men' (verse 14), which reflects the internal
disruption of the Hebrews church. Also the readers are to
strive for 'the holiness without which no one will see the Lord'.
The idea is perhaps indebted to the thought of the example of
Jesus, seeing that 'he who sanctifies and those who are
sanctified have all one origin' (2.11), but it is meant to apply to
holiness of life in general. Holiness of life requires avoidance of
both idolatry and sexual immorality. Idolatry is suggested here
by the reference to the 'root of bitterness' (see Deut. 29.18), but
the emphasis falls on immorality (cf. 13.4). Jewish ethical
thought held that visions of God could be obtained only in
conditions of sexual purity. Thus according to Jubilees 4.19–20
Enoch had his vision into heaven before his marriage. In Exod.
19.15 Moses commands the Israelites to observe sexual absti-
nence for three days in preparation for the theophany on Sinai
(which Hebrews will refer to in verses 18–21). Hebrews shares
the common idea that the vision of God is the goal of approach
to God (cf. Ps. 27.4, 7–9; Matt. 5.8). It is one way of speaking of
the direct access to God which has been established by the
inauguration of the new covenant. As so often in Hebrews, the
choice of a different concept acts as a bridge to the fresh
imagery needed for the grand description with which he will
bring the chapter to a close.

Another bridge concept is the return to dire warnings in
verses 16–17, using the example of Esau. This is another
allusion to contemporary Jewish ethical teaching, as Esau is
used as a model of unrighteousness, including fornication, in
several Jewish sources.[116] Here Hebrews chooses one well-
known moral lapse of Esau to show the fatal effect of failure to
persevere in the life of faith. Esau 'sold his birthright for a single
meal' (Gen. 25.29–34), and thereby lost his blessing (Gen.
27.30–40). It is thus implied that he sold his most precious
possession for the sake of immediate satisfaction, which is
exactly what the readers are tempted to do! Moreover, 'though

---

[116] Bruce, pp. 366f., cites *Jub.* 25.1; Philo, *Leg. All.* III.2 and *Quaest. in Gen.* IV.201; and
the *Midrash Rabba* (*Gen. Rabba* 70d, 72a; *Ex. Rabba* 116a).

he sought [the blessing] with tears' (Gen. 27.38), he had 'no chance to repent',[117] not because he had no change of heart, for indeed he was filled with bitter remorse, but because in selling the birthright he took a step which could never be undone. Such is the danger to which the readers have exposed themselves.

It should now be clear that the response of faith has two sides to it, and both are brought out in the splendid conclusion in 12.18–29. On the one hand it is a matter of living in the present in the light of the future, because the completion of God's plan of salvation has already been reached in the person of Jesus, though it still waits to be completed in us at the parousia. It is thus possible to give a glowing picture of the future fulfilment in terms of present experience, in which the future is anticipated by faith. This is what Hebrews does in verses 18–24. Taking the Sinai theophany as model, with all its terrifying portents, he describes the present in terms of arrival at Mount Zion. This is 'the city of the living God, the heavenly Jerusalem'. These designations for heaven are familiar to us from other parts of the New Testament (e.g. Rev. 21.1–22.5; Gal. 4.26), but are also found in Jewish literature of the time.[118] It is the place of direct access to God, but according to Hebrews that is available to Christians now. This explains the rather confusing list of the persons who belong to the city, who are described without regard to their relation to present or future. There are, of course, 'innumerable angels' around the throne of God. But there is also the 'festal gathering and assembly of the first-born' (RSVm),[119] which means the company of the converts on earth, 'who are enrolled in heaven' by having their

---

117 Literally 'place of repentance', as also in Wisd. 12.10, which may be in the author's mind here. Westcott cites classical parallels for the phrase.

118 At Qumran the community appears to be identified with the new Jerusalem in 4QpIsa^d (fragment of a commentary on Isaiah 54; Vermes, 2nd edn (1975), pp. 228f; 3rd edn (1987), pp. 269f.), but the detailed description in 5Q15 (2nd edn (1975), pp. 262–4; 3rd edn (1987), pp. 271–3), which like Revelation is indebted to Ezekiel 40–8, may refer to a literal new building in the Messianic Age.

119 The RSV text takes 'festal gathering' with the preceding clause (the angels), but NEB and most modern editors take it as coordinate with 'assembly' (*ekklēsia*, not used here in the technical sense of 'church'). My interpretation of the passage as a whole is in broad agreement with that of Peterson, pp. 162–6.

names inscribed in the book of life (Rev. 21.27). The idea of a
festal gathering reflects the Christian liturgy, which corresponds with the liturgy in heaven. The allusion to the book of
life takes the thought to the function of God as the future
judge, so this is mentioned next. The heavenly company also
includes 'the spirits of just men made perfect'. These are the
heroes of the past, whose perfection, i.e. participation in the
finished work of salvation, had to wait for the Christ-event (cf.
11.40). Naturally Jesus himself is mentioned next as 'the
mediator of a new covenant'. This was achieved by his death,
here referred to in words reminiscent of the argument in
9.13–15 as 'the sprinkled blood that speaks more graciously
than the blood of Abel'. All these things are available now in
the life of faith.

On the other hand the life of faith presupposes that the
transition from the present time of waiting to the actual future
fulfilment will not be long delayed. So those who respond in
faith will retain a vivid sense that their present blessings are
only temporary and that the permanent reality of the eschatological time will quickly come to pass. So finally Hebrews
makes this point with a fresh note of warning in 12.25–9. The
allusion to Abel effects the bridge from the preceding description of present blessings. There may well be a connection here
with the Jesus tradition, in which it is suggested that the
present generation must bear the entail of sin of all former
ages: 'The blood of all the prophets, shed from the foundation
of the world, may be required of this generation, from the
blood of Abel to the blood of Zechariah, who perished between
the altar and the sanctuary' (Luke 11.50–1; cf. Matt. 23.35).
According to Gen. 4.10 the blood of Abel cried out to God from
the ground, and this is referred to in 1 *Enoch* 22.6–7, where
Enoch sees the soul of Abel in paradise awaiting vengeance.
But the blood of Jesus 'speaks more graciously' in that it is the
atoning sacrifice of the new covenant, and now the point is
that the readers should not refuse this marvellous offer of
salvation. Mindful of the terrifying effect of the Sinai theophany, Hebrews warns them that God has promised an event
in which everything perishable will be destroyed (verse 26,

quoting Hag. 2.6).[120] Only that which is permanent in relation to God will survive. But that is 'a kingdom that cannot be shaken'.[121] So finally Hebrews recommends gratitude that this is what is promised. It is nothing less than the capacity to 'offer to God acceptable worship, with reverence and awe'. For 'our God is a consuming fire' (verse 29; cf. Deut. 4.24; 9.3). The saving act of Jesus does not alter God, but makes him accessible to us in spite of our human frailty and weakness.

Thus from a variety of points of view Hebrews has shown the response of faith as a full and satisfying programme for Christian believers. There is no need for specific ceremonies of purification, because all that is necessary for atonement has been done by Jesus. On the other hand those whose consciences are wounded by the sense of sin should remember that the atoning sacrifice of Christ is the central theme of Christian worship (13.15). Thus, instead of being enticed away from the Christian assembly, the readers should redouble their efforts to participate fully in worship, and indeed in all aspects of Christian life. In this way they will regain full confidence, and the debilitating sense of a stain on the conscience, creating a barrier to open relationship with God, will be removed. All they have to do is to imitate the faith of the original leaders (13.7), holding on to their confession of Jesus Christ, which remains 'the same yesterday and today and for ever' (13.8). The theology of Hebrews is firmly based in the tradition of the apostolic preaching. It is his belief that everything that he has

---

[120] This is not just rhetorical exaggeration, but the real expectation of many people in NT times, and helps us to understand the excitement of earliest Christianity and the urgency of Hebrews' message. Besides the biblical allusions quoted in the text, which are reflected in the contemporary apocalyptic literature, Gentile converts are likely to have been influenced by the Stoic idea of a universal conflagration. M. A. Williams (*The Immovable Race* (Leiden, 1985)) has drawn attention to the presence of this idea in Philo's writings, and it also appears in the Nag Hammadi texts (see Wilson, p. 235).

[121] This is the one place where 'kingdom' (elsewhere in Hebrews only at 1.8 = Ps. 45.6 and 11.33) is used for the coming age. It may well be a reminiscence of the teaching of Jesus on the kingdom of God, especially as the concepts of fire and judgment belong to his teaching in the wake of John the Baptist. For the modern study of the subject see the excellent short collection of essays, *The Kingdom of God*, ed. B. D. Chilton (London, 1984) and the large-scale treatment of G. R. Beasley-Murray, *Jesus and the Kingdom of God* (Exeter, 1986).

said about christology and the priesthood of Jesus and his atoning sacrifice is a correct explication of the tradition which he has received. The novelty of his presentation stems entirely from the need to reassert this in a particular and urgent practical situation, for which his help has been sought. Little did he realise the importance of his contribution to the development of the theology of the New Testament at a creative stage in the emergence of Christianity.

CHAPTER 3

Hebrews and the New Testament

UNITY AND DIVERSITY

Hebrews is a unique strand in the cord of early Christian literature. It comes from a church which cannot be identified with any of the churches represented by the other books of the New Testament. It has no direct literary links with the Synoptic Gospels, the Lukan writings, the Pauline Letters, the Johannine literature, the Pastoral and Catholic Epistles, and Revelation. On the other hand there are echoes of all these writings, however faint, inasmuch as all stem from the rise of Christianity as a distinct movement of people who acknowledge Jesus as Messiah and Lord. What binds the New Testament together is the common base in the confession of faith in Jesus. The primitive preaching of it was closely related to Jesus' own proclamation of the kingdom of God, and was presented in a form appropriate to the Jewish audience from whom the apostles themselves were drawn. As Christianity grew and spread beyond the confines of Judaism, inevitably there was development of doctrinal statement, and the social fragmentation led to differences of emphasis and modifications and additions in the light of local needs and new problems which had to be faced. This is the reason for the distinctive character of Hebrews itself.

Thus we should expect to find that there is both unity and diversity in the New Testament.[1] In this chapter I shall first try to give some idea of the fluidity of theology in the New

---

[1] See the important study of J. D. G. Dunn, *Unity and Diversity in the New Testament* (London, 1977).

Testament period so as to provide a broader perspective for our study of Hebrews. I shall then summarise the chief results of the exposition of the theology of Hebrews which I have just given in the last chapter, in order to show the unique contribution of Hebrews to the theology of the New Testament.

(a) It has long been recognised that the accession of Hellenist (i.e. Greek-speaking)[2] Jews to the church in the very early days had profound effects on the historical development of the church and the formation of Christian doctrine. This group consisted mainly of wealthy and devout Jews from the Diaspora, who had settled in Jerusalem so as to be near the temple and join fully in its worship. But for some of them at least the reality did not match up to their ideals of spiritual religion.[3] These would be a ready audience for the tradition of Jesus' radical criticism of the Law, which directed attention to the state of the heart before God. Also the gospel of the sacrificial death of Jesus, dealing with sin at the personal level of relationship with God, would call in question the value of the temple sacrifices. We have to remember that in any case the primitive kerygma presupposed the imminent parousia, giving a sense of urgency to the issues at stake. In this situation the preaching to the Hellenists could appear as an attack on the Law and the temple as such. This explains the furious opposition of the majority against Stephen (Acts 6.13). Many of the Hellenist converts fled to their old homes in the Diaspora (Acts 8.1), with the result that the wider evangelisation was undertaken under their influence. We can soon see a variety of attitudes towards the Law. Though most Jewish–Christians continued to observe the Law, it was not long before Gentiles were admitted into Christian fellowship without the requirement of circumcision and the Law. Paul attests the difficulties that could ensue in mixed congregations in which the Jewish members felt bound to observe the Law (Gal. 2.11–21). The Judaistic controversy represents a backlash of the strict Jews,

---

[2] There has been a lively debate on the meaning of *Hellēnistēs* in the NT, but Hengel has shown that the word in itself means no more than 'Greek-speaking': see M. Hengel, *Between Jesus and Paul* (London, 1983), pp. 4–9.

[3] Ibid., pp. 56–8; H. Räisänen, 'Paul's Conversion and the Development of his View of the Law', *NTS*, 33 (1987), 404–19, especially pp. 413ff.

who wished to compel Gentile converts to Judaise. In Hebrews, on the other hand, we have the opposite extreme, in which a Jewish–Christian church has abandoned the Law on principle, regarding it as superseded by the act of God in Christ. Here there is already discernible the deep rift between the Christian movement and the Jews who did not accept the gospel, which had ended in irreconcilable hostility between church and synagogue by the end of the century.[4]

(b) In the development of doctrine the crucial area is christology. In our survey of the relation of Hebrews to the primitive kerygma in chapter 2 we saw that this is the one topic which presupposes an advance on the earliest preaching. Hebrews has a Wisdom christology, which has its closest New Testament parallel in Col. 1.15–20. This had most probably been reached before the Hebrews Christians were evangelised, so that it formed part of the foundation teaching which they received (2.1–4; 13.7). It provided the means to relate Jesus, already proclaimed as the exalted Messiah/Son of God, to the cosmic plan of God, and so laid the ground work for the concept of the pre-existence of Jesus. It is very significant that there is no sign in Hebrews that this developed christology was a contentious issue, as this proves that it was not felt to be a threat to the cardinal Jewish doctrine of monotheism. Maurice Casey has pointed out that the same is true of the Colossians passage and the comparable Phil. 2.5–11, which do not presuppose that the statements might be controversial from a Jewish point of view, and like Hebrews are clearly based on Scripture.[5] But he has shown that it is not the same with John, written perhaps twenty or thirty years after Hebrews. Here there is direct accusation of breach of monotheism (John 5.18; 10.35). The pressure to deify Jesus has gone further in John than in any other book of the New Testament. The preser-

---

[4] The Gospel of John and Revelation also represent basically Jewish–Christian churches which do not observe the Law and are at loggerheads with the unbelieving Jews near the end of the century. Neither of them can be identified with the Hebrews church.

[5] In a seminar paper read at the Regional Seminar of the Society for New Testament Studies, Hawarden, April 1988. The paper is a preliminary study for his forthcoming book on the development of christology in the NT.

vation of monotheism thus became a major issue in subsequent doctrinal controversy. Also the humanity of Jesus was called in question by the end of the New Testament period.[6] Hebrews is notably insistent that his humanity is essential, both for his solidarity with the human race and for the reality of his sacrificial death.

(c) That Jesus died for our sins is a general presupposition of New Testament theology, but there is diversity in the ways in which this is understood. At the risk of grievous oversimplification one can say that for Paul the essential point is that the death of Jesus is the supreme act of the love of God for his people, in which Jesus bore their guilt in the shame of the cross and opened the way to renewal of life in the resurrection.[7] In 1 Peter the model is developed of the Suffering Servant of Isaiah 53. John sees the cross as the moment when the total unity of will between Jesus and the Father is decisively demonstrated, so that union with Jesus through faith brings the believer into union with God. For Revelation the death of Jesus is a moral victory with cosmic implications, for by it the power of Satan has been broken. There are, of course, overlaps of detail in these various presentations, and John shares the idea of conquest of Satan (John 12.31–2). Hebrews, however, has his own very special contribution to make, as we have seen, and this will be referred to more fully below.

(d) Earliest Christianity proclaimed Jesus as the Messiah in the sense that he is the agent of God for the general resurrection and final judgment which inaugurate the kingdom of God. Hebrews shares the primitive position which holds that the parousia is imminent. However, as the parousia was delayed, so there were various responses which can be detected in the New Testament. The problem caused by the delay has been exaggerated in some reconstructions of the New Testament period. In fact it does not seem to have caused a major crisis.

---

[6] The tendency to 'docetism' (i.e. the idea that Jesus, being divine, only seemed to be human and only seemed to die) can be seen as an issue in the Johannine writings and became prominent in many of the Gnostic systems of the second century. See Dunn, *Unity and Diversity*, pp. 296–305.

[7] See W. G. Kümmel, *The Theology of the New Testament* (London, 1974), pp. 185–205.

The reason for this is that it was never a simply future expectation, for the *present* position of Jesus as the exalted Messiah created a dialectic between the present and the future, the 'now and not yet' of salvation, and this holds good whether the time in between is long or short. To some extent life in the present under the lordship of Christ anticipates the future, and the gifts of the Spirit in the life of the church are signs of the eschatological outpouring of the Spirit prophesied by Joel (Acts 2.14–21). But even in the early period there could be problems. We saw that the problem facing Hebrews is comparable to the problem of the Thessalonians in 1 Thess. 4.13 when some of their number died before the parousia. Later we find increasing emphasis on watchfulness (compare Matt. 24.32–51 with Mark 13.28–37) and on the virtue of patience (James 5.7–11). The writer of the Pastoral Epistles seems to have settled for long postponement, and attests the fading of eschatological expectation in the later history of the Pauline churches. In John the dialectic of 'now and not yet' is maintained, but the emphasis is moving towards realised eschatology, i.e. the concept that the future blessings are realised now without regard to a future event. John shows this tendency in his substitution of eternal life for the kingdom of God. Even where the dialectic is expressed, the emphasis is on present experience (see John 4.23; 5.25). For Mark the eschatological 'hour' is still future and unknown (Mark 13.32). For John it is the cross (John 17.1).

Against this background it is possible to see that Hebrews makes a contribution to elucidating the dialectic of 'now and not yet'. If the death of Jesus is a sacrifice for sins in preparation for the coming judgment, it clearly has the effect of creating in the present a situation which belongs to the future, for divine forgiveness of sins is our only hope when it comes to the judgment. Hebrews shows in detail that this remains assured in the interval because of the continuing efficacy of the sacrifice of Christ.

CONSTRUCTIVE THEOLOGY

The earliest period of Christianity was a highly creative phase, in which all the principal positions of the primitive kerygma were worked out. Thereafter the major constructive developments can be plotted out in relation to the work of a few outstanding writers, notably Paul and John. Hebrews takes his place alongside them as a creative theologian in his own right.

(a) The long and sustained argument, running right through the letter, is a notable achievement in itself. The intellectual effort required to control the subject and present it cogently reveals the inner coherence and rationality of the apostolic message in a striking and original manner. Hebrews is faced with a loophole in the gospel of the death of Jesus as a sacrifice for sins, because it left the question of post-baptismal sin unresolved. It might have been possible to answer the question in a few words, but Hebrews has seen that the integrity of the gospel as a whole is at stake. In fact the problem is having the effect of drawing away the readers from their Christian allegiance altogether. In reply he has thought the problem through from the bottom and thereby produced a remarkable piece of constructive theology.

(b) The affiliation of Hebrews to the Hellenist converts represented by Stephen opened the way to a new slant on the claim that by his death Jesus had inaugurated the new covenant. The idea that the Law and the worship of the temple are superseded by the sacrifice of Christ is correlated with the transition from the conditions of the old covenant to the eschatological era in which the new covenant comes into operation. Hence all the regulations in Exodus and Leviticus are obsolete. On the other hand the Law retains its validity as the revealed will of God, as the prophetic element in Scripture declares in advance the conditions which belong to the new covenant. The idea of the new covenant is more fully exploited in Hebrews than in any other book of the New Testament.

(c) The rich use of Scripture in Hebrews carries forward the traditions of exegesis already established in Christian dialogue with Jews. Hebrews uses it creatively, as one who is steeped in the Septuagint and thoroughly familiar with Jewish methods of exegesis. He does not, however, use allegorical interpretation in the manner of Philo, or even historical typology.[8] On the contrary, he always works from what he considers to be the literal meaning of the text. The Law provides the standards that must be fulfilled if the death of Jesus is to be regarded as the final and all-sufficient sacrifice for sins. As this cannot be done by means of exact correspondences, Hebrews brilliantly seizes the essentials of the Day of Atonement, and shows how the death of Jesus has all the necessary qualifications for atonement sacrifice, even if the blood-ritual is only the fact of his death by crucifixion.

(d) The argument for the permanent efficacy of Christ's sacrificial death is a major contribution to the theology of the New Testament. The idea that Christ by his death has taken away sins is found in all the main strands, but usually it is merely a statement (see John 1.29; Acts 13.38; Rom. 3.25; Eph. 1.7; Col. 1.14; 1 Tim. 2.6; Titus 2.14; 1 Pet. 2.24; 1 John 2.2; Rev. 1.5). Paul and probably John think of the Passover in connection with Christ's death (1 Cor. 5.7; John 19.14). Usually the metaphor of sacrifice depends on the application to Jesus of the Suffering Servant prophecy of Isaiah 53. There is also likely to be allusion to the sacrifice of Isaac (Genesis 22) in John 3.16 and Rom. 8.32. But Hebrews alone tackles the subject comprehensively and systematically, so as to show not only how it can be claimed that the death of Christ was a sacrifice for sins in general, but also how its effect is continually operative from the point of view of the 'sin which clings so closely' (12.1) in the time between the crucifixion and the parousia. It may be that the argument is no longer valid for contemporary theology, but it is a brilliant and cogent argument within its own terms of reference.

---

[8] Whereas modern scholarship has largely repudiated the allegorical interpretation of Scripture, historical typology came into favour in connection with the Biblical Theology movement of the 1950s. It draws attention to correspondences between the action of God in the past and in subsequent ages, especially between the exodus and the saving work of Christ, thus showing a pattern of redemption in history. For discussion of the issues see G. W. H. Lampe and K. J. Woollcombe, *Essays on Typology* (London, 1957).

(e) A spin-off from this central argument is the unique presentation of the priesthood of Jesus. It has no echo else-where in the New Testament.[9] The notion of the Christian community as 'a royal priesthood' (1 Pet. 2.5, 9; see also Rev. 1.6; 5.10) is derived from the application of the metaphor to the chosen people of Israel in Exod. 19.6, and is not related to a theory of participation in the priesthood of Jesus. But for Hebrews the priesthood of Jesus is a most important element in his total argument. He values it as a metaphor of the representative character of the humanity of Jesus (2.17; 4.15). But he also argues that Jesus possesses a real priesthood, different from the priesthood of Aaron and the Levitical priests, but better than it in every way. This depends on his Messianic interpretation of Ps. 110.4 in 5.1–10. He regards this as essential, because only the high priest is qualified to perform the blood-ritual in the Day of Atonement, which he takes as the standard of sacrifice for sins. In fact his metaphorical use of the concept of priesthood in connection with Jesus is more important than the proof from the figure of Melchizedek, because it has a truly creative quality, derived from the model of the Gethsemane tradition, which has made it an inspiring ideal of pastoral priesthood in its subsequent development in application to the Christian ministry and the doctrine of the priesthood of all believers.

(f) The notion of the church as the pilgrim people of God, though much canvassed in some modern presentations of Hebrews, is not really a leading idea in the theology of Hebrews.[10] It is used as a metaphor in chapters 3 and 4, where the future hope is spoken of as 'a sabbath rest for the people of

9 Some scholars, e.g. Rissi, argue that the idea was already familiar to the readers because of the casual way in which it is introduced in 2.17, but this rests on a misunderstanding of Hebrews' rhetorical method (see p. 41 above). Though 1 Pet. 2.5 speaks of Christians as 'a royal priesthood, to offer spiritual sacrifices acceptable to God through Jesus Christ', Jesus himself is never referred to as the offerer of his own sacrifice in this epistle.

10 It is the leading idea of Käsemann's *Das wandernde Gottesvolk* (Göttingen, 1958, repr. 1961), but is taken up by D. Guthrie in his commentary without Käsemann's theory of Gnostic influence; see also D. Guthrie, *New Testament Theology* (Leicester, 1981), p. 778. There is no allusion to the wilderness wanderings in 13.13, because the reference is a further allusion to the ceremonial of the Day of Atonement (see p. 11 above).

God' (4.9). But the metaphor is not sustained in connection with the present life of the church elsewhere. Hebrews does not have a developed theology of the church. He thinks of it as the group of those who have been baptised into Christ, who are therefore the heirs of the promises made to the fathers. As such they are the people of God, and can be referred to as the house of God (3.2–6; 10.21) in line with Old Testament designations. The usual word for church (*ekklēsia*) occurs only in a quotation from the Septuagint in 2.12 (RSV 'congregation'). Hebrews also shows no development of an institutional ministry, referring only to 'your leaders' (13.17). It is probable that corporate celebration of the sacrifice of Christ took the form of the eucharist at the meetings for worship, but the allusive style of writing forbids certainty (10.25; 13.10–16).

(g) Finally Hebrews contributes a new definition of the virtue of faith as action in the light of assurance concerning the future. This is a valuable counterweight to Paul's use of faith, which is easily misunderstood as an attitude of passivity. Hebrews' concept also deepens the rather shallow discussion of faith and works in James 2.14–26. For Hebrews faith is an attitude which applies to the whole of Christian life. It is the response to the work of God in Christ, and provides the practical answer to the distressing problem of the readers in their consciousness of sin. Like all the theology of Hebrews, it is well based in the biblical tradition and contemporary Jewish ethical teaching, but it represents a creative rethinking of the concept in the light of the Christ-event, resulting in a fresh and arresting presentation which must have been most inspiring to the original readers.

So Hebrews undoubtedly makes a new and exciting contribution to the burgeoning theological understanding of earliest Christianity. It remains to consider how far his message is relevant today.

CHAPTER 4

The significance of Hebrews for today

BASIC PRESUPPOSITIONS

Hebrews is a most accomplished composition, written with great verve and rhetorical skill, and has an inspirational quality which gives it lasting value as a religious writing. But it remains true that it is in some ways alien to the modern reader, so that it tends to be neglected by those who read the New Testament for spiritual profit. The argument on the sacrifice of Christ also seems to be locked in the presuppositions of the past, so that its value for contemporary theology can be called in question.

One reason why modern readers tend to be put off Hebrews is the sheer difficulty of following the argument. Every reader can see that the author is building up a sustained argument, but it is hard to grasp it as a whole. I hope that the long exposition of it in the second chapter of this book has helped to overcome this problem, and shown successfully that Hebrews keeps a strong grip on what he is doing from start to finish. To succeed in following the argument is half the battle in seeking for the permanent value of Hebrews.

There are still likely to be other problems and I shall begin this chapter by considering some of them in the light of our previous study. This will provide the opportunity to relate Hebrews to current issues in religion and theology, and so to indicate the lasting importance of this truly remarkable composition.

The plan of salvation

Hebrews shares the conviction of earliest Christianity that God has a plan of salvation which is on the brink of completion. This raises two problems for modern people, because it presupposes that God is in control of history in a way that is difficult to square with our global perspective, and it raises again the question of the delay of the parousia, which called for attention in the last chapter. Both problems can be eased by adopting a dialectical approach. We shall see that Hebrews has a particular contribution to make from both points of view.

For the first point, a dialectical approach sees the concept of a divine plan of salvation in terms of the human apprehension of God. From this angle the story of human apprehension of God is at the same time the story of God's revelation of himself to humanity. This concept can embrace all religions and all history, but it also draws attention to particular moments of revelation which have special importance for human understanding of the divine. The idea of a plan can be deduced from seeing significant events in sequence, but the biblical tradition goes beyond this and makes predictions for the future on the basis of these experiences. The Christian claim is that the revelation of God reaches its climax in Jesus Christ. The Wisdom opening of Hebrews (1.1–4), placing Jesus in the line of the Old Testament prophets, and identifying him from the divine point of view with the creative Wisdom of God, is a viable theological statement of the dialectic which affirms that human apprehension of God and God's self-revelation are the reverse sides of one coin. Jesus gathers up the truths made known to the prophets and fulfils the predictions which belong to the divine plan. It is obvious that these very broad assertions amount to no more than a suggestive way of looking at one of the fundamental problems of religion through the eyes of Hebrews.

For the delay of the parousia the answer is already provided in the 'now and not yet' dialectic of the completion of God's plan in Christ, which nevertheless still awaits its consummation. A modern view frankly admits that the original conviction of imminent consummation in the parousia was mistaken, but the 'now and not yet' dialectic can make room for this correction. Hebrews has a special contribution to make in this connection, because his main preoccupation with atonement for sin, which is the crucial issue for the original readers, is solved in relation to this pattern. For Hebrews atonement has been effected once and for all through the sacrificial death of Jesus. It is therefore part of the 'now', something that belongs properly to the future but which has already been accomplished. In the consummation there will no longer be need for reconciliation with God. Hebrews asserts that that situation has already been reached through the sacrifice of Christ. But he is well aware that people will continue to commit sins in the time in between. But he will not allow a solution which reduces the sufficiency and finality of Christ's sacrifice, such as is implied by the reversion to atonement practices under the old Law. His solution is given in the long section on the response of faith (10.19–12.29) and in the specific exhortations in chapter 13. Building on the concept that the new covenant, which also properly belongs to the consummation, has been inaugurated by the death of Jesus, he can assert that a new and personal relationship with God has been established in which the barrier of sin has been removed (10.14–18). In practice this means that the person who has sinned does not have to seek how to restore a ruined relationship, but to accept the fact that the relationship cannot be ruptured on God's side. Then repentance, which is the same thing as renewal of faith in the dynamic sense which Hebrews gives to faith, renders the restoration of the relationship immediate. More will have to be said about this later, but the point here is that Hebrews has a positive attitude to the 'now and not yet' dialectic which has a bearing on the practical response to the Christian presentation of the plan of salvation.

The use of Scripture

The way in which Hebrews handles Scripture also seems alien to many modern readers. At first sight it can appear to be quite arbitrary. The Old Testament is treated as the Word of God, so that a citation of it is regarded as conclusive proof (for example the use of Ps. 110.4 to prove the priesthood of Jesus). At the same time the laws of the Pentateuch are held to be inadequate and obsolete. Nevertheless it seems that the sacrifice of Christ must conform to them, though in a better way. This is because the arrangements for the tent are held to be copies of the heavenly temple, but do not match up to the original, and so are useless from the point of view of final salvation. Of course this raises the question why the people of God had to be satisfied with such inadequate copies for so many centuries. The overall impression is that Hebrews operates in an enclosed world of meaning in which everything has to be related to the Scriptures in one way or another.

It is true that Hebrews needs to invoke Scripture at every stage of his argument. This is because nothing else will satisify the actual situation in which he writes. Hebrews shares with his readers the conviction that the Scriptures, especially the Law and the Prophets and Psalms, have absolute authority as the revelation of the will of God. The readers will not be persuaded to accept his argument unless it can be proved from Scripture. His method is logical, because, as we have seen above (pp. 50–5), he follows what he considers to be the literal meaning of Scripture. Prophecies of the future are taken to apply to Jesus as the Messiah and agent of God's eschatological salvation. The laws are superseded by the inauguration of the new covenant. On the other hand they are analogous to heavenly realities (Hebrews calls them copies on the basis of Exodus 25.40). This is because they deal with real issues in religion. The particular interest of Hebrews is access to the presence of God. This naturally exists in heaven, but on earth the tent as the place of the presence is only a model, and not the real thing. But the cardinal point is that the new covenant has opened up direct access as in heaven. This belongs to the consummation, when the distinction between heaven and earth will be done away, but is available now through the saving work of Christ. Thus the heavenly realities lie behind the present world order and continue beyond it. So the idea that present arrangements are mere copies should be seen as a way of expressing the contingent character of the present world order. Hebrews holds that through Christ there is access to a higher and eternal reality.

Because the laws deal with real issues, they retain their value as a source for moral instruction. So Hebrews, like Paul, never questions this aspect of the Old Testament. What is superseded is those aspects of the Law which concern the approach to God. But they still help to clarify the issues at stake. So for reconciliation with God Hebrews takes it for granted that the conditions of Old Testament sacrifice, particularly the Day of Atonement, define the nature of the subject. This was of course essential in view of the situation of the readers, but it is a logical position to take. So the literal meaning of the relevant laws provides the standard which must be adhered to if the sacrifice of Christ is to be regarded as an atonement sacrifice. It may still seem as if Hebrews is operating in a closed world of meaning, but this really underlines the importance of understanding the letter within its own terms of reference before it is applied to modern problems.

The atonement ritual

Though what has just been said provides justification for Hebrews' use of the ceremonies of the Day of Atonement in his exposition of the sacrifice of Christ, it is these details, and particularly the blood-ritual, which are most distasteful to modern readers and make them wonder why it should be necessary to apply them to Jesus at all. This is not just a modern problem, for we have seen that there was considerable criticism of animal sacrifice in the ancient world, both among Jews and Greeks.[1] In his book *Hebrews and Hermeneutics* Graham Hughes takes up this sense of alienation.[2] It could thus even be suggested that one of the aims of Hebrews is to show how the Christian gospel opens the way to escape from blood sacrifices, which could not be avoided in Judaism because of the implac-

---

[1] See p. 89 above and n. 89.
[2] G. Hughes, *Hebrews and Hermeneutics* (Cambridge, 1979), pp. 87–90, 124–30.

able authority of the Law, until the Jews were forced by circumstances when the temple was destroyed in AD 70.[3] Thus Hebrews shares the contemporary sense of alienation, and if in spite of this it seems alien to us now, we can look to it to lead the way towards a constructive reinterpretation which can renew faith at an acceptable level. However, though we have observed possible indications that Hebrews shared the dislike of sacrifices, it is not the issue with which he is really concerned. It is essential for his argument that the death of Jesus fulfils all the proper requirements for an atonement sacrifice. He uses the regulations for the Day of Atonement selectively, but brilliantly seizes the essential features needed for his purpose. So the readers cannot dispute his argument on the grounds that anything is missing from the sacrifice of Jesus.

It is important to realise that Hebrews is not just spiritualising the notion of sacrifice. This was done by Philo without repudiating the actual sacrificial system. Philo also knows of Jews who have given up the practice of the Law, because they regard their spiritual interpretation of it as its real meaning.[4] But for Hebrews the performance of the sacrifices under the old covenant was correct in its time, but they have now been superseded by the sacrifice of the new covenant. He is clear, however, that they were inferior precisely at the point which makes a spiritualising interpretation desirable. For the death of an animal is no substitute for the will of the offerer (10.4, 11). This is one reason why the sacrifice of the new covenant has to take a different form in which the will of him who is both priest and victim is the central feature. But even this is not the main point. It is only one aspect of the old and the new. For according to Hebrews the sacrifices of the old covenant were never expected to have the permanent effect, requiring no further repetition, which is the chief characteristic of the sacrifice of Christ. Simply spiritualising a system which needs constant repetition is not the same thing as performing a spiritual sacrifice once and for all.

---

[3] For the possibility that sacrifices continued after the destruction of the temple see p. 19 above and n. 26.
[4] See Philo, *de Migr. Abr.* 89–93.

We are thus driven back to the purpose of sacrifice, which is another point of difficulty for the modern mind. We are aware of the value of heroic self-sacrifice for a person or a cause, but that is really a different matter.[5] Hebrews is concerned with sacrifice as a means of reconciliation with God. This corresponds much more with the instinct to give a present to someone whom we have wronged in order to make amends, which is a well-known psychological need. The desire for a comparable reconciliation with God has its psychological counterpart in the need to be reconciled with oneself in the face of acute feelings of guilt. This may well be the case with the people addressed by Hebrews. The simple answer to this problem from a Christian point of view is the doctrine that 'Christ died for our sins' (1 Cor. 15.3), and the main argument of Hebrews is a striking and original exposition of precisely this point. But it only too easily fails to cater for the felt need which people have to do something practical so as to objectify their inner conflict of emotions. The Churches today make very little attempt to meet the need at this level, though the discipline of confession and absolution in a context of personal counselling remains valuable. But the general failure of Christians to see that a practical response is necessary is illustrated by the situation in Africa, where African converts frequently feel compelled to resort to sacrificing a chicken to the ancestors when their consciences are deeply troubled. Hebrews does have a practical programme to offer, and what is suggested in the section on the response of faith will repay careful reflection from this point of view.

The rigorism of Hebrews

This is not exactly a presupposition of Hebrews, but it is a feature of the letter which increases the sense of alienation felt by many readers. However, we have seen in connection with the relevant passages (6.4–6; 10.26–31) that Hebrews is not a harsh and unyielding person. He values the concept of Jesus as a merciful high priest (2.17; 4.14–16), and indeed has made a

[5] See M. Hengel, *The Atonement* (London, 1981), pp. 1–32.

positive contribution to the pastoral concept of priesthood. This is shown further by his reasonable attitude to human weakness in these passages, which appears also in 12.2 and in the tone of the general exhortation in chapter 13. The rigorism of the two passages in chapters 6 and 10 has to be seen in the light of the rhetorical structure of Hebrews. We observed how in both places Hebrews exaggerates the impossibility of renewal after apostasy because he knows that the readers have not actually committed it, but then immediately assures them that he knows that they would never do any such thing because he is terrified that this is what they will do! These passages are written with urgency and passion, and cannot be taken as a reliable guide to Hebrews' normal and considered moral position. They were seized on by Tertullian because he wanted support for his own rigorist position.[6] But they need to be seen in proportion, and should not be misused as scriptural warrant for a harsh and uncompromising attitude towards moral failings which have no real connection with the point at issue.

THE MESSAGE OF HEBREWS

If great caution is required in using Hebrews as a source for Christian morals, it only underlines the fact which has been apparent all through our study of Hebrews that it is not a general treatise, but an urgent letter addressed to particular people in circumstances that are very different from our own. It needs, as already observed, to be understood within its own terms of reference before any lessons can be drawn from it for today.

Modern methods of literary criticism may have some value here, but again it is necessary to strike a note of caution. Hebrews is not a narrative or a poem which has to be elucidated and appreciated, but is an appeal to particular people to revise their understanding of their Christian faith and to abandon action which is incompatible with it. Structural analysis, as practised by Ricoeur and Patte, may help to expose the dynamics of the argument, but cannot alter the actual message

[6] See p. 69 above.

of the letter.[7] On the other hand, recognition of the rhetorical devices which Hebrews uses has been shown to be essential to a correct assessment of his writing, and many passages have been wrongly interpreted through failure to realise this. Hebrews should always be read with an eye to the intended effect on the readers. This means that special attention should be paid to the emotional impact of what Hebrews has to say.

To grasp the message of Hebrews we should read it imaginatively, entering into the situation, and making the effort to *feel* the author's anxiety for the readers, his pastoral zeal, and his deep sense of responsibility for them. We should also try to feel his commitment to the apostolic faith, his love of the human Jesus as the model of pastoral zeal, and the ideal of priesthood (2.14–18; 5.2, 7–10; 7.26–8), and his burning conviction that the gospel that Christ died for sins according to the Scripture is true. This will then put the central chapters on the priesthood and sacrifice of Jesus into proper perspective. We have to remember that the argument has been constructed with the specific needs and assumptions of the original readers in mind, and is not necessarily cogent from a modern point of view, for of course few people can share the presupposition that the ritual of the Day of Atonement defines what is required for reconciliation with God. But the point of reading Hebrews with imagination and sensitivity is not to agree with the argument, which may be impossible if one does not share the author's religious beliefs, but to grasp what he really has to say.

Perhaps this may be summarised most simply by the double description of Jesus in 12.2, 'the pioneer and perfecter of our faith'. For this captures the essential theology of Hebrews without loss of its practical expression, which is so important for him. Jesus is the pioneer because he is human, and has trodden the way that everyone must tread, remaining faithful in time of temptation and offering his will to God even in death. This is the way that is set before the readers, and is one aspect of the response of faith. Jesus is also perfecter, because as the

---

[7] See D. Patte, *What is Structural Exegesis?* (Philadelphia, 1976); D. and A. Patte, *Structural Exegesis: From Theory to Practice* (Philadelphia, 1978); and D. C. Greenwood, *Structuralism and the Biblical Text* (New York and Amsterdam, 1985).

agent of God's predetermined will to effect salvation (1.1–4) the process has been completed in himself first through his death and exaltation to God's right hand, and is open to all who confess his name. They too will reach completion of the salvation process if they maintain faith, which is the active response to the assurance given by the inauguration of the new covenant.

All other aspects of the theology of Hebrews are subordinate to this central aim. He comes close to affirming the two natures in Christ, divine and human, and these are implied in what has just been said above, but this also shows that the aim of dogmatic definition for him is essentially soteriological and he is not interested in it from the point of view of theoretical christology.[8] This is equally true of his atonement doctrine, which is not intended to be a new theory, even though it is highly original, but is simply an explication of the received tradition in terms which the readers can understand and accept on their own presuppositions.

Similarly the idea of the priesthood of Jesus has two aspects to it which are related to the requirements of the argument in its real setting. It is first introduced as a metaphor, and this for many people is likely to be the aspect which has greatest value. But it is then taken literally in the proof that, as Messiah, Jesus is the eschatological high priest of the new covenant. The argument appears artificial and unconvincing, in spite of the brilliant deployment of the figure of Melchizedek, and the reason for it is not easily accepted by modern readers. Hebrews has to argue that Jesus is a priest, because according to the Law only a priest may offer sacrifice. This is one facet of his basic presupposition that the Law provides the proper definition of what constitutes an atonement sacrifice, which is essential to his argument. Thus in Hebrews the priesthood of Jesus is both a metaphor and more than a metaphor. This leaves a certain ambiguity which has had profound effect on subsequent Christian theology.

In the first place the metaphor of priesthood is presented in

---

[8] This observation agrees with the critical evaluation of NT christology in J. D. G. Dunn's *Christology in the Making* (London, 1980).

Hebrews with a rare understanding of the pastoral ministry, which has contributed a most valuable and inspiring concept of priesthood. It is the ideal for all Christians, inasmuch as all share in the priesthood of Jesus (cf. 1 Pet. 2.5, 9; Rev. 1.6; 5.10). It is also the model for individual ministers in their approach to their pastoral task. In the second place, however, Hebrews' insistence that the Levitical priesthood of the old covenant has been superseded by the priesthood of Jesus has been used to support the idea that Christ instituted a new priesthood, the Christian ministry, which exists to offer sacrifice, the eucharistic commemoration of the sacrifice of Jesus himself, often referred to as the sacrifice of the Mass. This was the cause of tremendous controversy at the time of the Reformation, which has left deep and long-lasting dissension between Catholic and Protestant in western Christendom. Hebrews was used by both sides. The traditional mediaeval view can be summed up in the words of the seventeenth-century Roman Catholic scholar Cornelius à Lapide. He takes up the idea of Christ's perpetual intercession in heaven (Heb. 7.25) and points out that at the same time on earth, 'through priests appointed by him, Christ continually offers even to the end of the world the sacrifice of the Mass'.[9] The Protestant view is expressed by A. B. Bruce in his book on Hebrews: 'Priesthood, sacerdotalism, sacraments turned into magic sources of spiritual benefit, have no place in true Christianity.'[10]

Before we take sides in the matter, we should remember that the analogy between the priesthood and sacrifice of the old covenant and the Christian ministry with its liturgical function of celebrating the eucharist was natural and almost inevitable at a time when theology emphasised the typological correspondences between the old dispensation and the new. It goes wrong only when false consequences are drawn from it. This did happen, and the Reformation was necessary to remove

---

[9] Quoted by B. Demarest, *A History of the Interpretation of Hebrews 7.1–10 from the Reformation to the Present* (Tübingen, 1976), p. 27.

[10] A. B. Bruce, *The Epistle to the Hebrews: the First Apology for Christianity* (Edinburgh, 1899), p. 438.

abuses, even if it must be seen as an over-reaction in some ways.

So long as the church was a movement within Judaism there was no tendency to refer to Christian ministers as priests, because the Christian ministry evolved in independence from the hereditary Jewish priesthood (cf. Acts 6.7). The analogy appears for the first time at the end of the first century in 1 *Clement* 40, but only in a general way. Though Jesus is described as high priest (36.1) in direct dependence on Hebrews, this is not brought into relation with what is said about the ministry. Presbyters were not regularly called priests (using Greek *hiereus* and Latin *sacerdos*) until the third century.

Similarly the tendency to call the eucharist a sacrifice (*thusia*) does not begin until after the New Testament period, though, as we have seen, it is very probable that the 'sacrifice of praise' in Heb. 13.15 is an allusion to the liturgy of the eucharist.[11] The first unequivocal reference to it as *thusia* is in *Didache* 14.1–3. The justification for calling it a sacrifice is that it is the celebration of the real sacrifice of Christ.

The analogy of the Levitical priesthood tended to support the idea of the church's ministry as a special caste alone qualified to handle the sacramental means of grace. The restriction of presidency at the eucharist to the bishop, or to presbyters as his delegates, was developed first on other grounds.[12] But the idea of an order of priests within the church, alone permitted to celebrate the eucharist, is often upheld

---

[11] The phrase is derived from Ps. 116.17, where it refers to the *tōdāh* sacrifice (thank-offering). Thus it is a sacrificial term applied metaphorically to the Christian assembly or eucharistic liturgy as the church's act of praise for the sacrifice of Christ.

[12] Though the evolution of the Christian ministry remains obscure because of the inadequacy of the NT evidence, it seems probable that local churches were run by a group of elders (*presbyteroi*) or overseers (*episkopoi*) as in the Jewish synagogue. One of them, normally the president, would be the celebrant of the eucharist. By the second century the designation *episkopos* is confined to the president as a higher rank than the presbyters, so making the separate order of bishops. The bishop remained the normal celebrant, and authority for presbyters to celebrate the eucharist was the exception rather than the rule and clearly understood to be delegated by the bishop until the third and fourth centuries, when the growth of the church made it necessary to confer this authority on all presbyters at their ordination: see F. L. Cross and E. A. Livingstone, *The Oxford Dictionary of the Christian Church*, 2nd edn (Oxford, 1974), p. 1123.

today on the basis of the derivation of the priestly office from the priesthood of Jesus as presented in Hebrews. A false consequence of this analogy was the mediaeval emphasis on the mediatorial function of the priesthood. If the priest alone can celebrate the eucharist, and is thought to have a special power to do so, and if the eucharist is the earthly counterpart of Jesus' perpetual intercession, and so is thought to be the sole means of applying the benefits of his sacrifice to the people, then it seems to deny the whole point of Hebrews, that through Christ the new and living way has been opened for universal access to God. Christians found themselves in the same position as Hebrews' readers, compelled to resort to the earthly priests and their ceremonials in order to find reconciliation with God. So at the Reformation Hebrews was used to denounce this aberration of mediaeval theology and all its practical consequences in priestly power over the laity.

The answer to this abuse is not to sweep away Christian ministry and the sacrament of the Lord's Supper altogether, as has sometimes been done, but to go back to the sources in the New Testament, and in particular to see what Hebrews has to say. It is encouraging to note that this is being done by both Catholic and Protestant theologians (for a Roman Catholic view the work of E. Schillebeeckx, *The Church with a Human Face* (1985), is specially notable). Hebrews certainly recognises the value of the ministry, which he refers to as 'your leaders', but they are not represented as indispensable mediators, but as those who help the faithful on their way by their pastoral ministrations after the example of Jesus himself, as is so splendidly suggested in 13.17. This ministry to the people of God includes the 'sacrifice of praise', in which our access to God through the sacrifice of Christ is acknowledged and vividly realised in the symbolic act of the eucharist. It is legitimate to speak of the sacrifice of the Mass in the sense that Christians join in celebrating Christ's sacrifice, make intercession in and through him who ever lives to make intercession for us, and open themselves to the power of his endless life.

Not surprisingly, Hebrews has constantly influenced the liturgical texts of the eucharist. This can be seen in some of the earliest liturgies that have come down to us. It has even been suggested that the liturgies came first, and that Hebrews is quoting from them! Though this idea had a certain vogue in nineteenth-century scholarship, it is not really tenable and is universally abandoned today.[13] The early Roman liturgy has a reference (retained in the Tridentine Mass but omitted from some modern revisions) to 'that which thy high priest Melchizedek offered to thee, the holy sacrifice, the spotless oblation'.[14] There is a superb use of the language of Hebrews in the Liturgy of St James, which is worth quoting in full:

We render thanks to Thee, O Lord our God, for that thou hast given us boldness to the entrance in of Thy holy places, the new and living way which Thou hast consecrated for us through the veil of the flesh of Thy Christ. We, therefore, to whom it hath been vouchsafed to enter into the place of the tabernacle of Thy glory, and to be within the veil, and to behold the Holy of Holies, fall down before Thy goodness: Master, have mercy on us: since we are full of fear and dread, when about to stand before Thy holy Altar, and to offer this fearful and unbloody sacrifice for our sins and for the ignorances of the people. Send forth, O God, Thy good grace, and hallow our souls, and bodies, and spirits; and change our dispositions to piety, that in a pure conscience we may present to Thee the mercy of peace, the sacrifice of praise.[15]

It is not only the ancient liturgies which show the influence of Hebrews. Modern hymns, like William Bright's 'Once, only

[13] The idea was canvassed by J. M. Neale in an article in the *Christian Remembrancer*, 39 (1860) (unsigned, but reprinted in his *Essays on Liturgiology and Church History* (1863)). It was taken up with enthusiasm by J. E. Field, *The Apostolic Liturgy and the Epistle to the Hebrews* (London, 1882).

[14] As noted above in ch. 2, n. 77. The fact that the Roman liturgy is the only early liturgy to include mention of Melchizedek is a further indication of the special connection of Hebrews with Rome.

[15] This is the Prayer of the Veil, said by the priest when he unveils the bread and wine in preparation for the *sursum corda* and eucharistic prayer, quoted in the translation of J. M. Neale. As the action is simply a matter of removing cloths from the sacred vessels, there is no real analogy to the entry beyond the veil in the Day of Atonement liturgy, but it is enough to suggest the symbolism. This prayer belongs to a comparatively developed stage in the history of the liturgy, when there is a tendency to provide a separate prayer for each action. On the other hand it is older than the introduction of the screen or iconostasis in front of the sanctuary, to which it might appear to be more appropriate. Note 'the sacrifice of praise' as a designation of the eucharist at the end of the prayer.

once, and once for all',[16] apply the theology of Hebrews to eucharistic worship. The final blessing and doxology in 13.20–1 has come into recent collections of prayers. It is also used as the basis for an Eastertide preface in the eucharistic prayer, for a final blessing in Eastertide, and for the collect for the Second Sunday after Easter in the *Alternative Service Book* (1980) of the Church of England.

In the blessing of 13.20–1 Hebrews himself gathers up his theology in a liturgical form. He here includes mention of the resurrection, which has always been presupposed, but has not been actually stated previously. He also introduces the image of the shepherd, which no doubt comes from traditional usage. This provides a fresh allusion to the pastoral concept of the priesthood of Jesus. On this basis Hebrews prays that his readers may have grace to live out the practical consequences of what he has recommended in his section on the response of faith. With these words this book may suitably come to its close:

Now may the God of peace who brought again from the dead our Lord Jesus, the great shepherd of the sheep, by the blood of the eternal covenant, equip you with everything good that you may do his will, working in you that which is pleasing in his sight, through Jesus Christ; to whom be glory for ever and ever. Amen.

[16] Included in *The English Hymnal*, 2nd edn (Oxford, 1933), 327, and many modern hymn books.

Further reading

COMMENTARIES ON HEBREWS

The following are the most serviceable commentaries for English readers. The commentary by Bruce is outstanding, and the more recent commentary of Wilson can be highly recommended. Both refer to the Greek text, but knowledge of Greek is not essential. Guthrie and Snell have the needs of beginners in mind. Among older commentaries Westcott is judged by Spicq to be one of the best commentaries ever written on Hebrews. Moffatt represents a radical critical approach. Both Westcott and Moffatt require knowledge of Greek.

Bruce, F. F. *The Epistle to the Hebrews*, New London Commentary, London, 1965

Buchanan, G. W. *To the Hebrews*, Anchor Bible, Garden City, 1972

Guthrie, D. *Hebrews*, Tyndale Commentary, Leicester, 1983

Héring, J. *Commentary on the Epistle to the Hebrews*, London, 1970

Moffatt, J. *A Critical and Exegetical Commentary on the Epistle to the Hebrews*, International Critical Commentary, Edinburgh, 1924

Montefiore, H. W. *A Commentary on the Epistle to the Hebrews*, Black's NT Commentaries, London, 1964

Snell, A. *New and Living Way*, London, 1959

Westcott, B. F. *The Epistle to the Hebrews*, London, 1889

Wilson, R. McL. *Hebrews*, New Century Bible, Basingstoke and Grand Rapids, 1987

The fullest treatment of Hebrews is given in the commentaries of Attridge (English), Spicq (French), Michel (German), and Braun (German), which are indispensable for advanced study. Braun's is a maze of detail, but short on interpretation, and is best used for reference. Spicq's is considered by many to be the standard work on Hebrews.

Attridge, H. W. *Hebrews*, Hermeneia, London, 1989

Braun, H. *An die Hebräer*, Handbuch zum NT, Tübingen, 1984

Michel, O. *Der Brief an die Hebräer*, Meyer Kommentar, Göttingen, 1936; 7th edn, 1978

Spicq, C. *L'Epître aux Hébreux*, 2 vols., Paris, 1952, shorter edition in Sources bibliques, Paris, 1977

THE THEOLOGY OF HEBREWS

There has been no systematic study of the theology of Hebrews in English since Milligan, but the following general studies of Hebrews will be found useful. Manson's essay was very influential among British scholars in reasserting the Jewish character of Hebrews against an earlier tendency to emphasise links with Greek thought. Nairne's study is suggestive, but too imaginative. Rissi (German) is a systematic study, but based on an interpretation of Hebrews which in my view leads to false conclusions. Hughes attempts to relate Hebrews to modern problems of theology, but his book is hard going. Käsemann sees Hebrews in relation to incipient Gnosticism.

Bruce, A. B. *The Epistle to the Hebrews: the First Apology for Christianity*, Edinburgh, 1899
Hughes, G. *Hebrews and Hermeneutics*, Cambridge, 1979
Käsemann, E. *Das wandernde Gottesvolk*, Göttingen, 1958, repr. 1961; ET *The Wandering People of God*, Minneapolis, 1984
Manson, William. *The Epistle to the Hebrews*, Baird Lecture, 1949, London, 1951
Milligan, G. *The Theology of the Epistle to the Hebrews*, Edinburgh, 1899
Nairne, A. *The Epistle of Priesthood*, Edinburgh, 1913
Rissi, M. *Die Theologie des Hebräerbriefs*, Tübingen, 1987
Vos, G. *The Teaching of the Epistle to the Hebrews*, Grand Rapids, 1956

SPECIAL STUDIES

Demarest, B. *A History of the Interpretation of Hebrews 7.1–10 from the Reformation to the Present*, Tübingen, 1976
Grässer, E. *Der Glaube im Hebräerbrief*, Marburg, 1965
Hay, D. M. *Glory at the Right Hand: Psalm 110 in Early Christianity*, New York and Nashville, 1973
Horton, F. L. *The Melchizedek Tradition*, Cambridge, 1976
Loader, W. R. G. *Sohn und Hoherpriester*, Neukirchen-Vluyn, 1981
Peterson, D. *Hebrews and Perfection*, Cambridge, 1982
Schröger, F. *Der Verfasser des Hebräerbriefes als Schriftausleger*, Regensburg, 1968
Synge, F. C. *Hebrews and the Scriptures*, London, 1959
Vanhoye, A. *La Structure littéraire de L'Epître aux Hébreux*, Paris and Bruges, 1963
Williamson, R. *Philo and the Epistle to the Hebrews*, Leiden, 1970.

Index of references

145

Index of names

152

Index of subjects

154

Made in the USA